Villains

How does a criminal subculture perpetuate itself? What do offenders themselves think about what they do? *Villains* provides a rare insight into local and family traditions of petty crime. It looks at attitudes to crime and law enforcement, and the relationship of those attitudes to the culture and community in which they are expressed.

In an entertaining and illuminating account based on participant observation and extended interviews, Janet Foster presents the voices of different generations of offenders, and examines the transition from adolescent street crime to adult 'hidden economy' crime. She also looks at why women have such a markedly different involvement in lawbreaking and explores exactly how deviancy is linked to the social construction of masculinity and femininity. *Villains* is a valuable ethnographic study of the people behind the stereotypes and the cultural forces at work within them.

Janet Foster is a Research Officer at the London School of Economics.

Villains

Crime and Community in the Inner City

Janet Foster

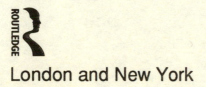

London and New York

First published 1990
by Routledge
11 New Fetter Lane, London EC4P 4EE

Simultaneously published in the USA and Canada
by Routledge
a division of Routledge, Chapman and Hall, Inc.
29 West 35th Street, New York, NY 10001

Typeset by LaserScript Limited, Mitcham, Surrey
Printed in Great Britain by
Biddles Ltd, Guildford and King's Lynn

British Library Cataloguing in Publication Data

Foster, Janet, *1961–*
    Villains: crime and community in the inner city.
    1. Great Britain. Urban regions. Crime
    I. Title
    364'.941

Library of Congress Cataloging in Publication Data

Foster, Janet, 1961–
    Villains: crime and community in the inner city / Janet Foster.
    p.   cm.
    Includes bibliographical references.
    1. Crime — England — London — Case studies. I. Title.
    HV6950.L7F66   1990
    364.9421'2—dc20   89–24177
                                              CIP

ISBN 0-415-02568-0

This book is for my parents Pat and Eric for always putting school before skating and for Mark who makes everything worthwhile

Contents

Tables and illustrations

Acknowledgements

Many people have helped me during the course of writing this book to whom, for different reasons, I would like to acknowledge my thanks. I am very grateful to Terry Morris and David Jenkins for supervising my Ph.D. thesis, on which this book is based, and to Paul Rock, whose assistance over the years has been invaluable. He deserves special thanks for ploughing through both my thesis and the manuscript several times!

The debt I owe to my family and friends is considerable. My parents have made numerous sacrifices over the years and I hope that this book will, in some small way, repay them. My husband, Mark, has provided endless support and encouragement and proved himself to be a very efficient editor! I would also like to thank David Wood for his assistance with some stages of the fieldwork, Lizanne Dowds for her comments on the introduction and Chapter 1, and Moira Parkes for doing the references.

I am grateful to the Howard League, who provided me with office accommodation for the duration of my research, and the Metropolitan Police for allowing me to observe and interview police officers at two stations.

Finally, and probably most important of all, I want to acknowledge my debt to the people whom this book describes. Their real names, for obvious reasons, cannot be used, but without their willingness to accept me into their world, this research would not have been possible.

Janet Foster
London School of Economics

Introduction

Little research has focused on what becomes of delinquents in adulthood. Indeed, crime is often viewed as an occasional, male, and teenage detour in an otherwise law-abiding life. Those who persist are seen to choose a criminal path at adulthood, while their friends desist under the responsibilities of marriage and fatherhood.

Research on 'youth' and juvenile offending burgeoned in the postwar decades with the emergence of teenage youth cultures which were regarded as new and entirely separate from the parent generation (Hoggart 1957, Nuttall 1968, Fyvel 1963, Cashmore 1984). Consequently little attention was paid to the possible continuity in experience, the transition from youth to adulthood, or the experiences and processes of change in the period from adolescence to adulthood and beyond. We know next to nothing about the attitudes of adults who offended in their youth, and whether these attitudes differ from, or reinforce, earlier experience.

The few studies which have pursued teenage offenders into their 20s and beyond (see West 1967, 1982, West and Farrington 1973, 1977, Glueck and Glueck 1940, 1968, 1974, Wolfgang *et al.* 1972) tend to have a heavily statistical emphasis (see Shover 1985 as exception). Autobiographies by professional criminals (cf Jimmy Boyle 1977, John McVicar 1974) offer insights into the more serious end of the offending spectrum but there are few accounts of the common petty offender. Yet this kind of offending is a prevalent feature of many communities, with institutionalised practices and attitudes associated with it (cf Downes 1966, Parker 1974, Gill 1977, Hobbs 1988).

It is these social worlds that exist 'somewhere between the underworld and the surface' (Hebdige 1977) which blur the models of juvenile crime and adult conformity so prevalent in the literature. Surely the settings where crime occurs, the experiences of adolescence, and whether these are sanctioned by peers, parents, and the local community all play a role in the persistence of attitudes into adulthood? These questions are rarely addressed by survey research, which is not designed to establish links between attitudes and behaviour or the cultural context in which these are expressed.

This book, based on eighteen months' participant observation and extended interviews in one area of South East London between 1983 and 1985, describes the experiences of two generations and their attitudes to law and order. It focuses on a middle-aged group of men and women who socialised in the Grafton Arms public house, and two contemporary groups of 'street-wise' teenagers. These individuals were not professional criminals but mundane and petty offenders, who graduated from a highly visible and public juvenile street life to the private, institutionalised exploitation of black economy outlets as adults. Their experience and manipulation of the social world of South London was strongly influenced by the area itself (perennially associated with crime and offending) which offered 'an excess of definitions favourable to the violation of laws' (Sutherland 1949).

Although participant observation is not a methodology which offers 'objective' and 'scientific' results, it provides an intriguing insight into the attitudes and values of a section of the population who rarely have a voice (and may not even appear in the 'official statistics' on which much existing research is based). Unfortunately, participant observation is also a time-consuming method and in offering an in-depth analysis of one group the experiences and behaviour of others are inevitably excluded. This book therefore focuses on a small group of white working-class men and women in one area of South East London. It does not describe in any detail the ethnic minority population who lived in the same area, whose perceptions, behaviour, and attitudes may have been entirely different. Their exclusion was not deliberate but resulted from the fact that none of the people that this book describes had any contact with minority groups in the area. Rather than engage in superficial analysis of a group whom I did not directly observe I have restricted my discussion of the ethnic minorities to the ways in which they were perceived by those this book goes on to describe. Clearly this is a one-sided account and in order to do justice to the ethnic minorities experiences is another and much needed book altogether.

For descriptive convenience I have divided the book into six chapters, four of which focus on different aspects of the research.

Chapter 1 provides a brief introduction to South East London, where the research was conducted, and highlights some of the factors in its history and development which have influenced patterns of crime and delinquency. Chapter 2 is the first of four detailed descriptive chapters and concentrates on the adult generation who congregated in the Grafton Arms. It introduces the main couples in the study and describes the semi-legitimate and illegitimate activities which took place there, and the attitudes, explanations, and meanings they attached to their behaviour. Chapter 3 provides case studies of three of the adult men and follows their 'careers' from youth to the present day. These indicate that attitudes and behaviour can often be at variance and that despite important transitions between youth and adulthood, attitudes altered very little.

Crime, as I noted at the outset, is regarded as a male pursuit. Chapter 4 discusses the role of women in working-class culture and suggests that the Grafton women did not become involved in crime because the 'delinquent solution' (Downes 1966) was less available to them. Their attitudes towards law-enforcement agencies are also discussed and the ways these were shaped by their husbands' offending.

Chapter 5 focuses on the younger generations, whose experiences strongly reflected those of the parent generation. It returns to issues raised in Chapter 3 on the transition from adolescence to adulthood, concentrating first on the 13–16 age group, and then the 17–19-year-olds, describing both the development of attitudes and the factors which influenced their behaviour during adolescence. A remarkable similarity in both experience and attitude was evident between the younger and older generations. This was not due to direct 'cultural transmission', but more subtle processes of parental reinforcement.

The final chapter draws together the differing settings and generational experiences described in the previous chapters, and places them within a wider perspective, considering how research based on ethnography might be used in considering avenues for change in the light of the marked continuity found in both experience and attitude.

To protect those who participated in this research, the names of all persons, streets, and places have been changed. For geographic and descriptive convenience I have divided the area into Gorer Lane and Stanton (see map in Figure 1). Like most other inner city areas they were depressing and run down. Gorer Lane was predominantly a white working-class area perennially associated with crime. Stanton was an area of increasing Afro-Caribbean settlement, which caused resentment and hostility amongst the indigenous white population, and was slowly transforming the character of the area and its population. Despite these changes, the subjects of this study, all indigenous whites, remained strongly tied to tradition. Informal and illegitimate activities were an intrinsic part of their lives, and attitudes towards crime and offending were firmly embedded in their culture.

Figure 1 Map of Gorer Lane and Stanton

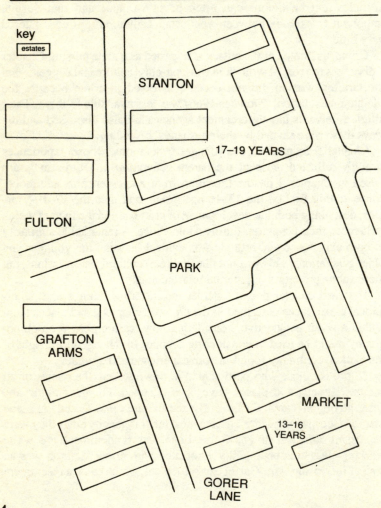

Chapter one

Crime, culture, and community

It may be said ... that the existence of a powerful system of criminal values and relationships in low income urban areas is the product of a cumulative process extending back into the history of the community and of the city. It is related both to the general character of the urban world and to the fact that the population in these communities has long occupied a disadvantageous position. It has developed in somewhat the same way as have all social traditions, that is, as a means of satisfying certain felt needs within the limits of a particular social and economic framework.

(Shaw and McKay 1942: 440)

Crime is an ever present and pervasive characteristic of many inner city areas. Poverty, unemployment, bad housing, and high population density are also perennial ingredients in the inner city jigsaw. In such environments distinctions between legitimate, semi-legitimate, and illegitimate activities are often blurred; attitudes towards crime and offending are more complex than clear-cut distinctions between 'right' and 'wrong' might suggest. Gorer Lane and Stanton, like many other inner city areas, have thrived on criminal activities for generations. Booth (1889) reported that the district was one of 'ancient ill-repute' at the end of the nineteenth century and this characterisation remains true to the present day, where some forms of crime are an institutionalised and unquestioned 'way of life'. As one local CID officer explained:

Almost everyone in this area has a criminal record or associates with criminals. Petty crime and receiving is a way of life. There is nothing wrong in it as long as you don't hurt anybody. Crime is almost inbred in generations here.

In order to appreciate how this situation occurred and to understand the 'cultural heritage' of which the two generations, described in this book, were a part, this chapter briefly describes the history of South East London and the patterns of crime and offending there. Its aim is to provide an overall framework for the detailed and descriptive analysis of the adult and youth generations which follow.

Old slums to new slums

South East London has to some extent always been regarded as the 'poor relation across the water' (Williams 1949) and did not develop significantly until the industrial revolution (because transport links with the city were extremely poor). As a result the area was for many generations largely isolated from other parts of London; even today, many South Londoners never go north of the River Thames (cf Bartles-Smith and Gerrard 1976). Although the area's geographical isolation and insularity played an important role in its development, the impact of the industrial revolution sealed South East London's fate as 'Huge areas degenerated from meadow to slum in a generation' (Bartles-Smith and Gerrard 1976). Descriptions of the area from the nineteenth century onwards were damning. Williams (1949) described it as 'a bad place, a sink of shadow and sorrow, vice and filth, ignorance and degradation' while Booth (1889) believed it was 'poverty stricken and overcrowded', 'inhabited by thieves, and unfortunates', 'a citadel of outcasts.'

These powerful images of the area as poverty stricken and crime prone remain an important characteristic in the twentieth century. Despite the fact that heavy bombing during the Second World War and the slum clearance programmes which followed changed the face of the area (about 50 per cent of housing is post war, OPCS 1981), many of the old slums were simply replaced by new ones. One police officer called the area 'the arsehole of the world!' another described it as 'absolute degradation.' (Foster 1989). Many share in their condemnation.

The 'utopian' ideals which influenced the erection of the huge system-built council estates that dominate the Stanton and Gorer Lane skylines today are now recognised to have been a dreadful mistake (cf Coleman 1985, Power 1987). Poor design and construction often combined with extreme social isolation for many of the estates' occupants. Slum clearance programmes disrupted kinship and community ties and although there is some debate about whether it was the effects of slum clearance itself or wider social changes which were taking place at the time that made these policies so unpopular (cf Parker 1973, Ungerson 1971, Mogey 1956, Coates and Silburn 1970) there is little doubt that slum clearance had a devastating impact on the Borough in which Gorer Lane and Stanton are situated. As one local explained:

When the big development and slum clearance started, these people were picked up and they were moved, most of them quite reluctantly out of their own areas, and although they only moved p'rhaps two or three miles sideways, it really just wasn't the [same]. . . . They moved these people and they were split up and rehoused – very few of 'em actually stayed in the Borough. [Therefore] all the estates were retopped with people from all over the place, the whole community got diluted down. You had a great influx of discontented people that didn't want to be living here anyway, but were rehoused and as a result the whole thing went down hill. Over a ten-year period this enormous movement left very little of the indigenous people of the Borough left, it just went and then you had people from everywhere.

This resident's impressions are given some support by Clarke and Hedges survey of the Borough in 1976. They found that only 17 per cent of those sampled had 'long term personal associations with the area.'

Despite the close geographical proximity of Gorer Lane and Stanton and a similar social and economic profile, post-war changes affected Stanton more severely than Gorer Lane and had a consequent impact on resident profile, ethnic minority settlement, and patterns of crime and offending there.

In Gorer Lane, while slum clearance influenced levels of community relations and neighbourly contact (cf Clarke and Hedges 1976), it remained a relatively homogenous area, as a police officer brought up there argued:

The average person from Gorer Lane was probably born and bred in Gorer Lane of stock that were born and bred here. [They] have always done a particular job.... They become road sweepers, they become dustmen, they go into the print. They take largely manual type work, semi-skilled work, because their dad did it and can introduce them.... The council provide the accommodation.

Stanton however was less resistant to change in the decades after the war and the effects of slum clearance itself seem to have been more dramatic there. The three huge council estates which dominate the skyline in East Stanton have become some of the most notorious in the country and experienced difficulties from the outset, as one local explained:

> When [the East Stanton] estate was built, ... people from practically all over London were moving in ... and I do believe East Londoners will not live alongside South East Londoners ... they don't communicate. They were rehousing people from far away on to that estate with people who were local and they didn't hit it off.

Hostility between Londoners was not the only area of conflict, as other immigrant groups like the Scots and Irish discovered. Their experiences were similar to those Stacey (1960) found in Banbury. She wrote:

> it may be said with a fair degree of certainty that working-class families from the north of England or from Scotland are very unlikely to settle on intimate terms as neighbours to Banburians (p. 110). ... To the Banburians the immigrants seemed 'foreign' ... because they came with values and customs greatly different from those of the town (pp. 14–15).

The new estates therefore began their existence with considerable difficulties but these almost pale into insignificance alongside the problems which have occurred since their habitation, many of which were due to poor architectural design. One report commissioned by the local council recommended spending £29.6 million to remedy faults on one estate which was only eleven years old. Certain kinds of crimes such as burglary were facilitated by split-level designs (cf Newman 1972, Brown and Altman 1981, Coleman 1985), whilst the rubberised walkways and badly lit corridors provided adequate opportunity and cover for 'muggings'. All these factors, in addition to the sheer numbers of people in a very small geographical area, soon resulted in the number of tenants requesting transfers far outweighing those wishing to move in. Inevitably they quickly became 'sink estates'.

The changing face of Stanton

While Gorer Lane remained a traditional white working-class district, Stanton became an area of Afro-Caribbean settlement during the 1950s and 60s (cf Glass 1960). Like other minority groups they were treated with hostility and prejudice but because they were also highly visible they became an 'identifiable enemy' who were blamed for many of the problems in the area and its decline.

As all the participants in this research were indigenous whites, who had no direct contact with black people in the area, the description which follows documents their attitudes towards the ethnic minorities and discusses some of the wider implications of minority settlement in Stanton. Clearly this is a one-sided account and the attitudes of both generations were extremely racist. While such attitudes were endemic in their culture it does not make them acceptable.

Although the presence of black people provided a convenient scapegoat for many white tenants in explaining the decline of Stanton, neither this nor their belief that the ethnic minorities received preferential treatment in housing allocation have any foundation. Research both in this country and the United States suggests that the ethnic minorities often receive the poorest and most inferior housing (CRE 1984, Rex and Moore 1967, Deakin and Ungerson 1973, Burney 1976, Lambert *et al.* 1978, Greater London Council 1976). Therefore Stanton, like other areas of minority settlement must already have been in considerable decline before the minorities arrived.

In many respects the Gorer Lane estates were no better than those in Stanton (one police officer for example described a notorious Gorer Lane estate as 'the bowels of the earth' housing 'evil people') but more of the indigenous white population seems to have been maintained. Although these patterns of settlement may have been influenced by local authority housing allocation policies (which was beyond the remit of my research to establish), structural factors such as the availability of local employment and geographic characteristics also influenced patterns of settlement. Yancey and Eriksen (1979), for example, found in Philadelphia that industrial areas with established working-class families were more resistant to minority settlement. Although blacks tended to live in the poorest areas of the city generally, they were less likely to live in industrial areas close to railways. Consequently 'It is the non-industrial areas which are most vulnerable to abandonment and subsequent invasion by blacks.' Gorer Lane was near to the railway, local employment, and industry, and was well served by transport to other areas. East Stanton had few of these assets.

The concentration of ethnic minority settlement in East Stanton and its relative absence in Gorer Lane was given a physical dimension by the creation of a large local park from the old bombsites and the disused canal. This area marked an important boundary between the estates of

East Stanton and those of Gorer Lane and created a 'defended neigh-bourhood' (cf Suttles 1972). Youths, for example, rarely went into or across the park, each kept to their own territory. The development of the park therefore in addition to other geographical features (for example the positioning of roads) emphasised the impression that Gorer Lane was 'white' and East Stanton 'black'. The division was real to residents and police alike, as an officer from Gorer Lane police station illustrates:

> There's so many white yobs here that the coloureds have been kept out. There's always a boundary, there are coloureds coming in down the bottom of the ground at Stanton's end, but it's just creeping on, it's not in the main blocks, very few coloureds, really, we don't get the problems with coloureds.

It is important to stress that these descriptions of Gorer Lane and East Stanton as areas with discrete boundaries are not, with the exception of the park, geographically accurate, but have a crucial symbolic importance. As Suttles argued:

> qualitative map[s] ... cannot match exactly or even closely the physical structure of the city. Usually, ecological distributions merge or shade into one another with no obvious break. For example people may describe three adjacent areas 'white', 'black' and 'mixed', although in fact each racial group simply shades off into the other. In this sense, one's taxonomy of the city represents a creative imposition on the real world. It is not unrelated to the real world but translates it to another scale.
>
> (Suttles 1972: 32)

Although, as I have argued, ethnic minority settlement did not cause the decline of Stanton, it did have a crucial influence on indigenous tenants' willingness to remain in the area. A local newspaper report on the first black man to move on to one Stanton estate aptly summarises both the fear and hostility directed at black people who moved into the area. One tenant said, 'I do not like the idea of coloured people on the estate, which is a nice place at the moment.' Another said: 'God knows what we'll find in the evenings now ... one hears so many awful stories!' Other tenants argued: 'Life will be hell' (South London Press, 1964). The local home beat police officer who worked on one of the estates at the time told me:

There was a tremendous influx of coloured families on the estate and I think it has to be said that many of the families did not want their kids to grow up with coloureds for neighbours.

Feeling threatened and 'swamped', many of the white tenants sought transfers. This often proved impossible due to the low status of the estates, as the numbers of tenants wanting to move off far outweighed those willing to move in. Consequently many tenants who had been born in the area and had considerable links with it reluctantly moved to other parts of South East London (cf Fernando and Hedges 1976), once more influencing patterns of interaction and kinship. As one resident remarked:

A lot of people on the East Stanton estate when it was first opened were the type of people who lived in council accommodation and they were council people . . . but they moved in and they couldn't get to another area [so] people sat down and said:'Right we're gonna buy our own property' and they moved out to Welling, to Sidcup, anywhere in Kent.

Another said:

They moved out in little jumps until some people got so paranoid that they just want to go somewhere which is completely and utterly immigrant free and they don't care where they live or how much it costs them.

It would be absurd to suggest that migration resulted entirely from ethnic minority settlement in East Stanton, especially as home ownership has become much more common among skilled manual workers in post-war years (cf Hamnett 1986: 18). Nevertheless after more than twenty years of minority settlement racist attitudes show no sign of abating; the regulars in the Grafton Arms felt that the presence of black people had made a 'decent existence' impossible. Joanne, for example, who moved out of the area during my research, argued:

Where we're moving, a friend of Billy's lives across the road and he was saying 'It's a different life here all together, there's not one black', but that's everybody saying that. My sister will say 'There's not one black in my road', but that's a big thing not to have one. A few years ago it used to be 'Do you know there's a black living in our road' and that was surprising. But now it's a big thing not to have one.

Whilst Sal said:

> My mother has never had to say to us, 'Right we're moving out
> because there's nowhere for us to live decently' and we've had a
> decent life. She would never have said that. Yet now we've got to
> say it because we've got to move out. It's terrible, I'd love to live
> round here forever and ever but I just know it's my kids or their
> kids.

'Community' and kinship in South East London

Although the effects of post-war changes in East Stanton were more
dramatic than those in Gorer Lane, slum clearance did contribute to a
weakening of kinship networks and 'community' life in both areas. The
old slum neighbourhoods, however poor, were often seen to be
supportive environments where most people knew one another and
would help each other out. Yet, as Bartles-Smith and Gerrard point out,
slum dwellers

> had contrary to popular belief little sense of community
> involvement and belonging. It was, when it existed, a united sense
> of common deprivation. . . . They had no stake in the area. Even in
> the early twentieth century when the community spirit was
> strongest, when fewest people had moved and immigration had
> ceased, the sense of identity was not based on anything they
> owned, . . . but on their mutual deprivation. Constantly the best
> emigrated. Their leaving created a ghetto for those who could not
> depart.
>
> (Bartles-Smith and Gerrard 1976: 25)

Notions of 'community' are often idealised and unrealistic (cf Pearson,
G. 1983). Yet there is a powerful belief that 'community' is a good thing
that is often lacking, particularly in anomic and unneighbourly high-rise
council estates. Although such images are not always correct (see Foster
1988) there have been significant changes in patterns of kinship and
association in the area as a whole. As Clarke and Hedges (1976: 12/158)
pointed out in their study of the Borough:

> we were struck by the extent to which people felt that the large-
> scale post-war redevelopment . . . has destroyed what might be
> called 'community spirit'. . . . What people mean by community
> spirit however, is difficult to pin down. To some older people it is

likely to be nostalgia for the past, for a sense of community probably only possible among people facing problems of poverty which were often endurable only when shared. Now what remains in the memory is the closeness engendered by the sharing of hardships, rather than the bitterness of poverty. However, a sense of community does seem to exist in many areas and where it is thought to be declining rapidly much regret is expressed.

Clarke and Hedges found that 'only two in five' residents in the sample felt 'they belonged to a community'. East Stanton was perceived to be the 'least pleasant place in the borough to live' and had the lowest degree of community spirit (see Table 1). Nevertheless kinship ties remain an important feature of the area (cf Clarke and Hedges 1976) but are rarely characterised by common residence on a particular street or estate (see Table 2). Wallman's observations in South West London are equally appropriate to Gorer Lane:

Table 1 Levels of community feeling

	All Households Base 2073 %
Feel part of community	39
Do not feel part of the community	(61)
Believe community exists	15
No community exists	38
Don't know if community exists	8

Source: Clarke and Hedges 1976: 159

Table 2 Location of friends and relatives

	Location of friends and relatives		
	Mainly in same district	Live half in district and half elsewhere	Mainly elsewhere
Base: Seen some socially in the last seven days	918	329	669
	%	%	%
Feel part of the community	47	46	29

Source: Clarke and Hedges 1976: 162

It is clear that most of the south London born are well placed in terms of access to kin as a local resource. The elderly have children and special relatives nearby for company and support. Sons and daughters are able to rely on parents and other relatives for advice and practical help. Their local kin networks include various generations and consequently their knowledge of and information about the area are likely to be extensive and effective. The latter point shows very clearly in relation to acquiring employment.

(Wallman 1982: 115)

These aspects of kinship ties and friendship networks will be discussed in Chapter 4, as women in working-class culture play a major role in maintaining family connections (see Young and Willmott 1957, Klein 1965, Wallman 1982). For the moment it is important to emphasise that despite all the changes which have taken place around them, the lives of those described in this book remained rooted in tradition. For them Young and Willmott's famous characterisation of Bethnal Green remains salient:

Either length of residence or localized kinship does something to create a network of local attachments, but when they are combined, as they are in Bethnal Green, they constitute a much more powerful force than when one exists without the other. Then people have a number of links, or ways of orienting themselves, to the same person: he was at school, he is a relative by marriage, he lives in a well known neighbourhood. The people can make use of one or the other of their possible approaches to establish a relationship with almost anyone. . . . In this old established district the relatives are a vital means of connecting people with their community. The family does more than anything else to make the local society a familiar society, filled with people who are not strangers.

(Young and Willmott 1957: 116)

The traditions of crime in South London: a league division of villainy

The preceding historical discussion provided a brief account of the area's development from the industrial revolution to the present day and illustrated that, despite dramatic changes in the geography of the area, many of the 'traditional' elements of working-class life still remain. Tradition also played an important role in both attitudes and patterns of offending in the area and it is to these issues which I now want to turn.

The two most celebrated examples of South London villainy in the twentieth century were the Great Train Robbers and the Richardson brothers (Parker 1981, Lucas 1969, Read 1984). The Train Robbers captured the hearts and imaginations of thousands of working-class people when they robbed a mail train in 1963. Read (1984) in his biography of the men argued that their lives must be seen within a context of a 'whole sub-society of working class South London', where 'there is no doubt that there was and is still endemic poverty juxtaposed to conspicious consumption north of the River.' He describes the robbers as showing 'total repugnance for the rules and formalities of the modern state' where 'the only authority recognised by (them) was the natural authority of a "name" - another criminal who had earned their respect through demonstrable qualities of courage, cunning and ruthlessness' (1984: 321–2)

Organised crime stood at the top of a 'league division of villainy' in the area, which one police officer likened to a football league division table, where involvement in criminal activities occurred simultaneousely on a variety of levels.[1] The 'league table' is divided into three basic groups: the 'real' villains (division one); the 'honest' villains (division two); and league division three villainy. These divisions represent highly simplified 'ideal types' and reflect both traditional aspects of crime, which remain an important characteristic of the area, and more recent patterns of offending which have resulted from the dilution of traditional community and kinship networks in Stanton, and other forms of crime, for example drugs, which have become more prevalent. The characteristics of the different leagues are outlined below:

The real villains

I have a certain amount of respect for those who have a life of crime because they hold their own moral codes, and have a concept of a fair cop, which is more than can be said for the slags who kick in the front door and burgle all their neighbours.

(Police Officer, Stanton)

Although a large proportion of crime in both Gorer Lane and Stanton was of a relatively petty nature, the area has always attracted a number of professional criminals. As one officer commented:

> There's a lot of good villains living on this ground. You get a lot of yobs who are full of mouth and everything else, but you get a lot of good villains. . . . They don't do petty burglaries, they'll do armed robberies, like the bullion thing.

It is this professional element who comprise the league division one catagory. They are characterised by their readiness to use actual or threatened violence in the commission of their crimes. As Read notes:

> When Gill Hussey asked Jim, who she considered so gentle and controlled, how he had come at the age of 18 to beat up a police inspector he had simply replied, 'It's the name of the game'. Buster's defence of the coshing of Mills, was that he did 'what had to be done'. It is the logic of the profession which in criminal careers leads to cruelty and death.
>
> (Read 1984: 325)[2]

While it is often assumed by law-abiding elements that those who engage in crime have no morality, it would be misleading to suggest that the violence of 'professionals' is totally arbitrary. One of Hebdige's respondents aptly summarises the situation

> Straight people say that the people who are beneath the law live in the jungle. But there's a law of the jungle. It's like a religious code. If you are involved in the twilight zone there are certain rules laid down and you abide by them.
>
> (Hebdige 1977: 30)

This was illustrated to some extent by the activities of the Richardsons, who headed the South London underworld during the 1950s and early 1960s. Parker, in his excellent biography of the brothers, wrote of the violence which led to the famous 'Torture Trials':

> To most people, these attacks were brutal. In terms of the south London code and sub-culture, they were not much out of the ordinary. Both men were villains anyway, both had had their share of fighting and violence. They had taken a liberty and they deserved what they got. . . . 'It was just one of them things,' says Roy Hall today, 'They took a liberty. We got the hump. They got a whack.
>
> (Parker 1981: 198)

Parker rightly points out that although such codes exist, we must not fall into the trap of believing that they are always applied; rather they are general guidelines which are breached from time to time. Parker highlights the contradictions between theory and practice in the trial of Charlie Richardson.

> The saddest thing about it is that Charlie really felt he was innocent. The Old Bailey trial had dealt solely with the cases of the few men who had been beaten. To Charlie, they had deserved what they had got. They were con-men who had tried to take him on. Their beatings were permitted in the underworld code by which he lived. But even if some of his victims were con-men – some in fact had not taken Charlie on at all – they were not men of violence. Neither had Charlie's violence been spontaneous. It had been premeditated, almost savoured in its anticipation.
>
> (Parker 1981: 337)

Only one person discussed in this book fell into the 'real villain' category but the influence of the group was marked in two ways: first the knowledge of their existence and behaviour acted as a marker for the other groups in assessing their own criminal behaviour and the codes of conduct which they employed; second their presence provided a communal sense of pride, and those who had managed to 'beat the system' were regarded as 'heroes'.

Honest villains

The second league division of villainy involved the 'Honest Villains' who operated according to similar codes of conduct to the professionals but began from the premise 'there is nothing wrong with crime as long as you don't hurt anybody'. Violence in this instance was more a threat than an actuality and where it did occur tended to be restricted to summary justice. This was an important characteristic of working-class life in general. Distrustful of the police and feeling that summary justice often had much more impact (in terms of personal satisfaction and a greater deterrent value) it was a regular occurrence in the area. As a detective constable pointed out:

> Gorer Lane's ground still has a lot of real old South London people that 'sort out their own problems'. If you went to a fight the victim signed a statement saying that they didn't want the police

to investigate the incident. Later the person responsible for the assault got a pasting and the same reply would come. 'Don't worry Guvnor, no police – we'll deal with it in our own way.'

The influence of the area and its local employment structure had an important effect on crime where certain trades (for example in second-hand cars and scrap metal) offered ample opportunities for dealing in stolen goods (cf Hebdige 1977). The Richardsons, for example, used their Peckford Scrap Metal company as a front for many of their illegitimate activities (see Lucas 1969, Parker 1981), and in this study, Del, the most successful person with whom I had contact, was a scrap metal dealer who bought and sold stolen goods (see Chapter 2). Offences which fell into the 'honest villainy' catagory included fraud, fencing, certain types of burglary, theft, and shoplifting.

Whilst the first two categories of villainy encapsulate some of the traditions of the area and its crime, the third includes elements of change which were perceived to be increasingly threatening by both police and criminals alike.

League division three villainy

40 per cent within the Borough you could almost class as league division threes or potential league division threes and drugs is largely responsible for it. . . . Twenty years ago you didn't have a drugs problem.

(Police Officer, Gorer Lane)

The third division represents the vast majority of offenders and includes three distinct types of offending: the unsuccessful and inadequate law breakers who were without skills and persistently got caught; drugs and drug-related offences; and finally street robberies ('muggings') and other activities identified as 'black crime'.

The proliferation of both drugs and mugging in recent years was a threatening development because it created instability and unpredictability in certain parts of the area – East Stanton in the case of 'black crimes' (see Table 3), and the large white estates in Gorer Lane in the case of serious drugs such as heroin. Both these forms of offending tampered with the relationship which existed between the police and the criminal fraternity, as one officer explains:

The average villain in this area had a lot of respect for us. We're on the other side of the fence, but it's a game. . . . They're honest in as much as you know where you stand with them. League division three criminals you have problems with. They are the types who hit back, the ones who will never accept nothing ... you don't know where you stand, you've gotta watch yer back the whole time. If I know where I stand that makes all the difference. Funny thing to say about a villain but it's the only way I can adequately describe it.

Although both offenders and law enforcers recognised the existence of a 'game' in some of their interactions, offenders were always at a competitive disadvantage and often had little choice but to participate in it (cf Carlen 1976). Nevertheless the existence of this understanding between the police and the criminal fraternity involved a degree of negotiation and acceptance of each side's position (cf Parker and Allerton 1962).

Table 3 Total number of recorded offences Jan–Nov 1985

	Gorer Lane	Stanton
Violence against the person	298	177
Street robberies	178	237
Other robberies	129	151
Burglary – dwelling	1,583	1,130
Burglary – other	689	493
Theft and handling stolen goods	4,521	2,973
Theft of a motor vehicle	565	422
Unauthorised taking of M/V	859	409
Theft from motor vehicle	1,498	960
Theft from person – snatch	283	149
Theft from person pickpocket	136	51
Fraud and forgery	257	184
Criminal damage	1,251	969
Total	11,247	8,315

Source: Gorer Lane and Stanton Divisional Plans, Metropolitan Police

Although I have described these different divisions as being mutually exclusive, there is of course movement within the hierarchy. Juveniles, for example, would begin in league division three but might progress into the top division, although this avenue was restricted to a reasonably small number of people. Many more negotiated an existence between the semi-legitimate and illegitimate spheres available in both 'honest' and league division three crime.

To my knowledge, contact between the different divisions was limited due to differing networks and beliefs, but a degree of interaction did occur between the second division and other groups (see Chapter 2). I have used this hierarchy of villainy as a crude analytic tool to provide a framework within which to consider the attitudes and behaviour of the people now described.

Summary

This chapter has provided the reader with the historical and descriptive background of Gorer Lane and Stanton. The local history reveals a tendency towards isolation from other areas of London, a tradition of local employment, and a perennial association with crime. Although slum clearance led to some dilution of community feeling, the extended family network remained important. Despite dramatic geographical change the character of Gorer Lane and its residents has altered very little. By contrast, Stanton experienced greater transformation and immigrant settlement. A 'league division of villainy' was used to describe the differing levels of crime which occurred simultaneously in the area; divisions one and two were linked to attitudes and behaviour firmly rooted in culture. Division three contained changing patterns of offences which were perceived to be increasingly threatening to the relationships between the police and certain sections of the criminal fraternity, the stability of the neighbourhood, and patterns of victimisation. Crime then both of a petty and organised nature was a way of life for many in the area which, as I will illustrate in the following chapter, was generally condoned.

Notes

1 I would like to thank Chief Inspector Davies for this league division analogy, which I have expanded and developed.
2 There is some controversy about the exact definition of a professional criminal. Mack (1964) suggests that violence need not be an integral aspect of professional crime, while Taylor (1985) argues that only a very small number of criminals (possibly 500) throughout Britain actually possess 'professional' status. This title is reserved for those involved in serious and organised crime, for example armed robbery.

Chapter two

The Grafton Arms

> Some public drinking places derive their special character from the fact that they are used as though they were not public places at all, but rather as though they were the private retreat for some special group.
>
> (Cavan 1966: 205)

The first chapter provided a brief discussion of the theoretical background to this book and an outline of the area where the research was conducted. The forthcoming chapters focus on differing aspects of the area of South London which I observed, beginning here with the adult generation in the Grafton Arms. It describes the pub and the locals who frequented it, the 'business' which was conducted there, and the attitudes towards law and order which Del and his friends held. Many of the characteristic elements of South London described in the last chapter were prominent features among the Grafton community and, as the discussion here will illustrate, certain forms of crime were an endemic and accepted way of life.

Surrounded by two large and notorious council estates, in a generally depressed area of South London, one would have been unlikely to wander into the Grafton Arms by chance. Despite a large ethnic minority population the pub's clientele were almost exclusively white and working class, many having lived in the area for three generations. In a background of physical decay, high unemployment, and deprivation, the pub mirrored what was outside its doors – it was dreary and sparse. In the public bar the barest of necessities were provided: a fruit machine, dart board, and a few wooden tables and chairs. In the carpeted lounge bar, a picture of the Queen rested above the fireplace and the heavily patterned velour wallpaper was old and faded.

The pub, given its position and interior, did not attract passing trade and had few attractions for the young, who tended to go to the more up-market pubs and nightclubs with late-night licences. As a result the Grafton's clientele were a relatively static group of middle-aged people with a few elderly regulars.

Pubs have traditionally been the domain of male working-class culture (Harrison 1943, Gorham and Dunnett 1950, Klein 1965, Dennis *et al.* 1956, Hey 1986) providing a welcome escape from the problems of daily life (Harrison 1943, Cavan 1966, Gill 1977). As a result work was rarely a topic of conversation in the Grafton since the men, either self-employed in manual trades, such as painting and decorating, or employed in skilled and semi-skilled occupations like scaffolding, engineering and printing, tended to work long hours: evenings were seen as a release from such rigours.

The Grafton was not only a means of escape. It hosted both ladies' and men's darts teams, who played competitively in a local league and also provided a forum for regulars to do business, where anything from council flat keys to cheap videos or washing machines could be acquired. Pubs often play an important role in the exchange of stolen goods (Mars 1982), and the aspects of 'doing business' and the methods of exchange will be discussed later in the chapter.

Bar territory

The clientele in the Grafton Arms reflected some of the divisions which were apparent in the area itself. These were expressed both in the physical use of bar space (in a division between public and lounge bar territory) and in the differing attitudes and values of sections of the clientele. Although there were notable exceptions, remarkably little interaction occurred between clients in the two bars. Figure 2 indicates the use of bar space by the different groups in the pub.

Those of Irish and Scottish origin, in addition to the 'Teapots', all occupied lounge bar territory. While at first sight this might appear the superior of the two, with its more comfortable and carpeted interior, the public bar, where the darts board was situated, was in fact the most coveted space. The Scots and Irish (most of whom were second generation) used the pub because of both its convenient location near their homes and the absence of any black people. They were to some extent considered 'outsiders', with differing attitudes, networks, and connections than the public bar group. The strength of these networks

Figure 2 The clientele of the Grafton Arms

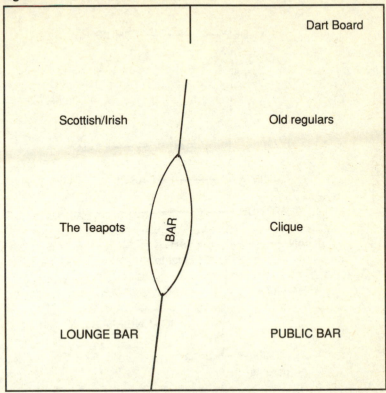

was important in demarcating leadership of the darts teams and influence within the pub itself (see Figures 3 and 4).

The 'Teapots' were indigenous South Londoners, but never used public bar territory. Their title was derived from the amounts of alcohol they consumed. Del said of the 'Teapots':

They were ... born and bred here. Most of the Teapots are brothers... there's four or five brothers and they've just evolved around that. . . . There's only ten of 'em I s'ppose and they're very close knit . . . I don't really know their full background but I think they've had a spot of 'bovver' at one time or another, which makes 'em that close knit. . . they very much look after each other. If one's in trouble they're all in trouble or the rest will get the other out of trouble. . . . If you're a Teapot you're a Teapot one hundred per cent.

Figure 3 Social networks and relationships in the Grafton Arms

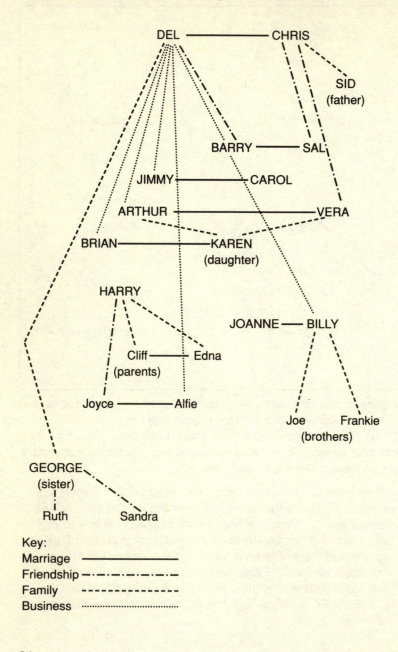

Figure 4 The ladies' and men's darts teams

The ladies' darts team

Michelle (32)	Captain* (Scottish)
Sue (28)	Michelle's sister.
Chris (37)	Responsible for recruiting most members, hence importance.
Sal (37)	'Fetched in' by Chris – had been friends since teens.
Vera (40)	Rarely played for the team but was always present at games. Drank only with Chris, Sal, and Carol
Carol (33)	
George (22)	So named because of her boyish appearance – Del's sister.
Ruth (22)	Worked with George
Sandra (19)	Recruited by George

The men's darts team

Harry (mid-30s)	Captain*
Del (37)	
Barry (35)	
Jimmy (34)	
Billy (28)	
Joe (31)	
Frankie (34)	
Paul (19)	The only youngster to play in the team, Paul was a talented player who spent most of his time with Jimmy, but also played pairs in another pub (which was run by one of Arthur and Vera's daughters) with Chris.
Scottish Dave (40s)	The only non-indigenous Londoner in the team.

* This position did not carry any status with it, since the captain's job was mostly an organisational one which involved attending meetings etc.

Given the exclusivity of the Teapots and the nature of their activities they had little interest in extending their group. Del was the only member of the public bar clique who had honorary status and influence with them.

The demarcation of territory in the pub also reflected the differing attitudes of the two groups: the 'honest villainy' and institutionalised crime in which Del and his counterparts were involved, expressed as 'normal' since it seemed that 'everyone did it', contrasted with the more unsavoury and distasteful division three crimes which were supported by the lounge bar clients. These differing attitudes were clearly illustrated when a local newsagent and his wife were severely beaten during a robbery. A television news report watched by regulars in the pub on the evening of the incident highlighted the different attitudes of the two groups. Those in the public bar expressed a mixture of disbelief and revulsion at the extent of the injuries, whilst those sitting in the lounge bar expressed faint amusement and indifference. It transpired later that some of the lounge bar clients knew the people responsible for this incident.

In addition to the darts clique the public bar had a few elderly regulars, most notably Harry's (the barman) parents, Edna and Cliff, and Mary, an elderly woman who drank there most evenings. Edna and Cliff occasionally played darts with the clique or cards and dominoes with another couple, whose son was a police officer (see p.45).

The group which dominated the public bar, however, was the darts clique. Comprised of the central members of the ladies' and men's darts teams (see Figures 3 and 4), the clique included the publicans Arthur and Vera, Del and Chris (the person who introduced me to the group), Carol and Jimmy, and Barry and Sal. The discussion and description in this chapter concentrates on these couples. It was they who held the central focus of attention within the pub, both in terms of their relationships and within the darts teams themselves.[1]

On evenings when the ladies' darts team played at home (once a fortnight) the public bar was occupied entirely by women and the men were relegated to the lounge bar, but on other nights the pub was largely a male domain. There was little place in this culture for a single woman in her early 20s without a man and soon after the research began, when I was invited to mixed gatherings, it became important that my presence was neutralised by the existence of a man to whom I was attached and therefore 'unavailable'. As a result I was sometimes accompanied to the pub by Dave. He easily gained access to the male culture (which my gender excluded) and being an artist was able to provide particular services (see p.31).

Five couples formed the caucus of the public bar group and they are described in detail below.

Vera and Arthur

Vera and Arthur were the publicans of the Grafton. Both had lost interest in the pub as their continued applications to the brewery for money for improvements had been refused. Arthur, a thick-set man in his early 40s, had a rather dishevelled appearance. He was a heavy drinker, and was often drunk and abusive to both Vera and customers.

No one seemed to know anything about his background but there were rumours that he carried a 'shooter'. Vera was slightly built and about the same age as Arthur. She was a bitter and abrasive woman, with an acid tongue. She resented the spectacles that her husband made of himself, which both angered and embarrassed her and as a result they always rowed. Del and Chris were their closest friends and Arthur, who once owned his own cleaning business (but went bankrupt), worked for Del during the research. They had two daughters, one of whom ran a local pub, the Sussex; the other lived with Brian (38), who worked for Del. Vera and Arthur also had a young son John (16), who had just left school.

Chris and Del

Chris and Del were the most important couple in the pub and seemed an unlikely match. Del was small and slight while Chris was tall and well built; he was quiet and softly spoken, she was more lively and outspoken. It was Chris (37) who introduced me to the Grafton and facilitated much of the information and co-operation I gained there. She held a central position in the ladies' darts team and was unusual in the degree of interaction she had with men in the pub.

Del (37) was the most likeable character in the Grafton. He was an unassuming man and was very successful in terms of South London working-class culture. He owned three businesses, in addition to interests in a pub and several chalets in a seaside resort. Such enterprises had made him relatively prosperous: 'Seven years ago I didn't have two bob, people'd steal off me now' he said. Well liked and respected, he was known amongst those in the Grafton as someone who both bought and sold stolen goods and was often sought out by people and interrupted while playing darts to 'do business'.

Barry and Sal

Barry and Sal were also an unlikely couple. Barry was small but well built and had an image of himself as a fighter. He sported several tattoos from a period in the army, told numerous war stories, and tended to exaggerate. Sal was a tall and rotund woman with a good sense of humour. She was the most detached member of the darts clique and expressed many attitudes which were more typically middle class. She found ladies' night 'boring' and said she would much prefer to do things with Barry than alone. Sal did her best to try to moderate Barry's behaviour ('he's always in head first, I'm hangin' back and thinkin' about it, that's the difference between us') but essentially she and Barry had fundamentally different outlooks. During an interview Sal told me:

> Go out and see life before you get married, before you get tied down with responsibility, get your education, do like you're doin', go and get yourself a decent job, go and see a bit of life before you get tied down.

Barry's response was 'Shit, if you want it go and get it'.

Carol and Jimmy

Carol and Jimmy, who were slightly younger than Chris and Del, had a significantly different life style from most of the other couples. They lived in a pre-war two-bedroomed council flat with their two young children, in conditions which Chris accurately described as a 'slum'. Both had been married previously and at the beginning of the fieldwork stood out from the other couples in their overt show of affection for each other. Sadly their relationship declined over the months.

Jimmy (34) was a small, slim man who had learned very little from his mistakes. Although he had aspirations to be rich and was very impressed with the trappings of success, Jimmy would never be able to attain them. Even his 'fiddles' were not very successful.

Like many other women in this culture, Carol, Jimmy's wife, had a very hard life. She once described her mother's experience thus: 'she grins and bears it' and much the same could be said of Carol herself. Carol was a shy but affable person who always looked thin and pale and appeared much older than her 33 years. The strains of working and bringing up the children (2 and 5) almost single handed had taken its toll. She drank heavily on occasions to drown her problems and her voice had a coarse quality due to the number of cigarettes she smoked. Her relationship with Jimmy was aptly characterised by him: 'I wouldn't swap what I've got now for all the tea in China, if she'd swop me or not, she most probably would given half the chance.'

Billy and Joanne

Billy and Joanne were relative newcomers to the pub, as they used another 'regular' until Billy was banned after a fight. Billy, in his late 20s, was grossly overweight and not well liked due to his aggressive attitude and treatment of Joanne. Joanne was also obese but smaller in stature and quiet by nature. Although often humiliated by Billy in the pub Joanne never made any attempt to defend herself. She told me: 'I know there's a lot of give and take, but there's a lot of putting up with things. I put up with a lot for a quiet life. . . . Like I'll let him go to darts more than once a week, but then a lot of times if he's home we don't talk, so he might as well be out.'

Joyce and Alfie

A catering manageress, Joyce was bawdy, loud, and talked incessantly. She played darts for the Sussex because the Grafton women did not want her in their team but this snub did not prevent Joyce's frequent visits to the pub. She could be found most nights of the week propping up the bar. Joyce's presence was tolerated as she had known Harry (the barman) for many years. Her husband Alfie was a mechanic. Although he was always with Joyce in the Grafton he rarely spoke.

Harry

Harry was the regular evening barman. Although he had a full-time job, he worked in the Grafton most nights of the week and often spent his non-working hours there too – either way he drank heavily. Harry's role as barman was important because, like Del, he had contact with all the clientele. Captain of the men's darts team, Harry had a menacing appearance and looked like a stereotypical villain. He was never seen without several pieces of heavy gold jewellery which, he said, were acquired as a reward for doing some 'shady business'. He had served a long prison sentence for grievous bodily harm on his girlfriend. Harry claimed that he was a professional hit man for the South London underworld and was said to have several 'shooters' indoors.[2]

'Doin' business': networks, dealing and profit

'It is not accidental that pubs have long been traditional places in which to do amateur business. Custom is predominantly local and customers can . . . be positively vetted . . . relationships are informal.

(Mars 1982: 174)

'Doin' business' was taken for granted as an integral aspect of life in the Grafton Arms and like other accounts of hidden economy trading (Ditton 1977, Mars 1982, Henry 1978, Hobbs 1988), goods were often obtained from work-related practices. Jimmy, for example, worked in a bakery and regularly provided Arthur with food for the pub.

> When I used to work for ... we used to nick bleedin' sausage rolls, pies, pasties, flour, eggs, chips, meat, literally everythink .... Arthur used to have 'em in the pub.

Ditton argued that these activities were part of a 'hidden economy' where

> Merchandise is regularly and 'invisibly' stolen, covered, transported, exchanged, purchased and consumed in ways that never 'come to light'. The 'hidden economy' may be defined as the: 'Sub-commercial movement of materials and finance together with systematic concealment of that process for illegal gain.' The hidden economy is a microcosmic, wry reflection of the visible economic structure upon which it parasitically feeds. ... The 'hidden economy', then, runs to the 'side' of the legitimate.
> (Ditton 1976: 275, quoted in Henry 1978: 5)

Unlike Ditton, Henry (1978) maintains that hidden economy activities are not as extensive or profitable as they might first appear. To some extent this was reflected in some of the 'business' transactions which occurred in the Grafton. However, neither the economic and 'parasitic' model suggested by Ditton, nor the limited amateur trading networks observed by Henry, fully explain the motivation, nature, and variety of business in the Grafton.

Although some kinds of business were open to anyone who used the pub, it was most often conducted among those who were trusted and perceived as having the 'right attitude'. Business generally took two forms: service and reciprocal. Services were usually an exploitation of the workplace and occupational skills. Jimmy, for example, made darts. He stole the material from work and often used their lathes to fashion the metal. At £10 a set the team acquired custom-made darts and Jimmy got a 'tenner in his pocket'. Joe, a council caretaker, had an arrangement with Arthur about passing on the keys of empty council flats which could then be squatted. This too was done for a fee. Services sometimes had dual motivations, as in the case of Mo, who disconnected electricity for a living but, for a small fee, fiddled meters. He argued this compensated for the detestable nature of his employment for which he felt unpopular and ostracised.

Business transactions were not always assessed in financial terms because many were based on reciprocal favours (cf Henry 1978: 33-4). Barry, for example, distinguished between dealing with Del, which was a reciprocal relationship, and 'business':

> I wouldn't buy nothink from Del's yard. Cos I don't buy it, if it's for me I go down and see Del and it don't cost me nothink. I mean we're friends simple as that. . . . If Del comes to me and he wants some scaffolding for the yard then I'll do it and it won't cost him a penny.

But at the garage, another of Del's businesses, this was not the case as it was run by someone else. Barry continues,

> Down the garage, it's a business, he's got another guy running it, so if he wants it done. . . I've got to treat that as a business and I will charge him and Del will pay.

Some 'favours' in the Grafton were done simply for the 'price of a pint'. Harry's daytime job in the paper industry gave him the opportunity to pilfer large amounts of paper and sketch pads of various types. As an artist, Harry felt Dave could make use of his goods and after he had been subjected to a testing phase with invitations to utilise his skills (painting a stock car for Del and portraits of two couples' children for which he was paid), Harry made the following overture to him one evening in the pub.

> You're the artist aren't you, you're the one who done those paintings for Del? . . . That's my line of business, do you pay for yer paper, what do yer use, cartridge, how big, pad, looseleaf? . . . Just tell me what you want, give me a few days and I'll get it for yer.

Harry ended the conversation by saying 'It won't cost yer nothink, just a pint'. Mars (1982: 174) argued 'If money is the medium of exchange in material dealings, drink is often the medium of exchange in personal dealings.'

The importance of reciprocal favours was not their 'material worth' but their role in 'fulfilling the expectations and moral obligations of the friendly relationship' (Henry 1978: 99). Therefore once people had entered into such dealing they were expected to reciprocate. This fact might only become apparent when a breakdown in the relationship occurred (cf Liebow 1967, Whyte 1943, Gans 1962). In the Grafton this was most clearly bought to light by Jimmy when Del sold him a car at a generous discount. As Jimmy had financial troubles Del assured him that he would accept whatever he could pay at the time and settle the remainder when he was able. Jimmy gave him £65 and said he would pay the rest the following week, but Del received no more money. Jimmy got into serious debt, stole the darts team's 'subs' money, and wrote Del a cheque that subsequently bounced. He was then sacked from work for thieving so Del found him a job in a local pub where he had business interests, Jimmy was caught 'dipping' in the till, and was sacked again. Not surprisingly Jimmy quickly fell out of favour as he failed to fulfil his obligations and made no appearance in the pub for several weeks. Nothing was done until he was seen driving a new car of recent registration around the area and was thought to be minicabbing. Del had still received no payment for the original car and yet another cheque had bounced. He sought retribution. Del explained that it was not the issue of the money but the fact that Jimmy had taken 'liberties'. He told me:

> In the beginning when I met him through darts, [it] always seemed that he had the right attitude, because he didn't know yer he didn't take any liberties with yer. But I found as soon as he got to know yer then the liberties started coming from that and it just snowballed.

The differing positions of Jimmy and Del in the Grafton are aptly summarised by Gans, who wrote:

> The highest status accrues to the person who makes the most material and non-material contributions to the group, without using these to flaunt or to indicate his economic or cultural superiority. Conversely, the lowest status is reserved for the 'bum', a person who cannot or does not want to function properly within the group. This term may be applied ... to an adult who fails to take care of his family, [and] to one who does not pay his debts.
>
> (Gans 1962: 27)

I witnessed only one business transaction with an outsider in the Grafton and, because such practices were entirely out of character, the exchange provoked much attention and comment. A young man in a blue trench coat with a white-patched Staffordshire terrier came into the pub and asked Harry if he would change a bag of money. He produced a large carrier bag filled with coins. The wad of notes he was given in return indicated that there was a considerable sum of money in the bag. The man was about to leave the pub when Harry poured him a half pint of bitter, indicating that he should stay. The man paid for his drink and drank it perched uncomfortably on a stool. Everyone present in the bar watched this exchange. Billy wryly commented 'I hope that aint my gas meter' whilst Sal remarked, 'It's nice to have friends isn't it.'

The operation of the informal economy

Now that I have outlined some of the ways in which business was conducted in the Grafton, I would like to discuss a number of issues where previous accounts of the hidden economy conflict with my own observations. First the label 'hidden' in itself suggests that these practices are actively concealed. Whilst at an official level, particularly in an occupational setting, this may be true, one of the characteristics of 'fiddling' at work is that management are often aware of and accept these practices (cf Dalton 1959). As Hebdige argues:

> Every job has its dubious 'perks', every factory its own sharp operators, its very own 'fence' who, with a wink and a whispered caution keeps his pockets lined and his friends supplied with cheap stockings for the wife and perhaps a few valuables will fall, with miraculous regularity, off the back of passing lorries. In some of the smaller workshops and warehouses and most of the big building-sites, the 'fiddles' have been formalised. Even the foreman plays his part in shifting stock off the premises. . . . Blind eyes are turned in every direction and blindness is endemic at half past five.
>
> (Hebdige 1977: 9–10)

Despite the large amounts of money sometimes involved in these practices employees are rarely reported or prosecuted (Dalton 1959, Martin 1962). Jimmy describes the pilfering which occurred in the bakery where he worked – both the security guards and his supervisor were involved.

Jimmy: When I used to work at . . ., we used to nick bleedin' everythink. Our freezer was full all the time. . . . Now you're talkin' about four years ago [1980] and I was bringing home most weeks £160 or £170 a week, I had some weeks when I've been bringing home £230 a week. I used to bring home gateaux that was the size of birthday cakes.

Carol: I had one of the lowest shopping bills in Stanton, it was lovely I used to go and buy steak for dinner, I had nothing else to spend the money on.

JF: So how did you get the stuff out then?

Jimmy: Just call a cab, see the security man. The security men, well ridiculous, there was three of 'em . . . Sunday's there was no production until after seven o'clock that night to make bread for the following day, so one of us'd come in the morning, or we'd both come in the morning and one of us would leave after the pub. If we both stayed we was on an earner.

JF So did you pay the security bloke?

Jimmy: Oh no, Tom or whoever it was, 'I'm calling a cab send him down to me', 'Hold on mate', in the boot, 'See yer later Tom.' He couldn't wait for us to go so he could do it hisself.

Most studies of amateur trading argue that because 'fiddling' occurs within an occupational setting, participants are involved in the hidden economy only on a 'part-time' basis. It has been assumed, therefore, that these 'actors', save for their occasional exploits, are in all other ways law abiding. The role of networks, the prevailing attitudes within them, and the areas where the hidden economy thrives receive little attention (see Hobbs 1988 as an exception). The hidden economy therefore is often discussed in a cultural vacuum. In the area of South London which I observed and the East End which Hobbs describes, the informal economy is an intrinsic part of working-class culture. People learn from an early age to exploit their environment using legitimate or illegitimate methods. The semi-legitimate and illegitimate, however, have distinct advantages: easier access, more likely fulfilment, and greater excitement (see Sykes and Matza 1961). For the clientele in the Grafton Arms there was no convenient dividing line between illegitimate, semi-legitimate and legitimate activities; as they were all an integral part of the existence of people in the area, not 'peripheral' and 'occasional' episodes in otherwise law-abiding lives.

Del's business serves as an example. He was more than an amateur trader. Known both by the police and local people as someone who bought and sold stolen goods, crime and receiving were just another aspect of his work. The scrap trade, long associated with all forms of villainy, offered Del an excellent opportunity to buy and sell stolen goods. Any opportunity which presented itself was exploited. He dealt with family, friends, and thieves alike and operated in a relatively small contained world where there were lots of other Dels, some bigger, some smaller. It is to a discussion of Del's 'business' which I now want to turn.

Del's business

> If they want somethink, they'd probably think of me before they think of anyone else. If they wanted to get rid of stuff, then I'd be on par with three or four others.

Del was the central figure in the Grafton because of his business connections, contact, and influence with all groups. His persona was very different from the 'Arthur Daley' image of second-hand car dealers and scrap metal merchants so characteristically portrayed. He was a quiet, unassuming man, who always remained slightly aloof from other regulars: 'I like to be in company out of company,' he said 'I look in on what's happening rather than being part of it', but Del was always on the look out for a deal: 'I don't like to see any way of making money go by, I've gotta have a go at it' and said his grandmother taught him early in life that if he could get a bargain from a pin to a battle ship, to buy it.

Del saw his business role in the pub as providing a kind of service which gave him pleasure but, he felt, gained him little respect.

> I like the feeling where people go, 'Where can I get 'em' and they go 'Oh Del'll get you it.' I like that feeling that I can do it and I can get it for 'em. But I don't think that gives me any respect cos I can get it like that. As I say all they're concerned with is 'Thanks, could yer, can yer?'[3]

As business transactions tended to be private and people avoided interrupting or disturbing those 'doin' business', this clearly made direct observation difficult. However, Del describes below the kind of transactions and conversations that were encapsulated in Chris's frequently uttered comment 'he's doin' business'.

It could be anythink I mean, tonight, a guy selling a pair of shoes – no one could afford to sell a pair of shoes for five quid, but the guys in the pub can. . . . In pubs there are always people that have got cars, they always want 'em repaired, or they want 'em to go from here to there (insurance fiddles, transport etc) every aspect of business. If someone came up to me in the pub . . . [and] said, 'I want a painting', automatically I'd think of Dave and I'd go, 'I can arrange it.' Therefore it now becomes business, that way I'd be lookin' at Dave sellin' his paintin' for £15, I'd be sellin' it for £20. I wouldn't think yeah Dave wants 15 quid, yeah I've got a pal who'll do that for 15 quid, that wouldn't enter me head – it's gotta be 'yeah 20 pound, he'll do the picture for yer.' But I'd be on £5 of it.

(Interview)

Del's comments may cast some light on the debate about the role financial gain plays in the hidden economy. Although some aspects of business were clearly of a reciprocal nature, Henry was perhaps a little naive in his interpretation of the lack of financial reward involved in the hidden economy transactions he observed (Rock 1987). Although, in actuality, transactions never realised their financial potential (see Hobbs 1988 for some amusing examples), the motivation for involvement was due to an orientation towards, and pursuit of, easy money (see Chapter 3). Del serves as an excellent example of the confusions engendered by the language of the hidden economy, arguing on the one hand that he was always on the look out for a deal and on the other that receiving was not a lucrative enterprise.

You've obviously got to have the money or they ain't gonna come to yer. Financially it never is, you always think it is at the time but it never does really. The ordinary car thief will go out and nick a stereo set out of a car, he might come to yer with five and three of 'em don't work, but you've paid for five, so it's all false economy.

This statement would support Henry's argument:

In its simplest form, hidden-economy trading is the illicit buying and selling of 'cheap' usually stolen goods that goes on among ordinary people in honest jobs. Unlike professional fencing, where the businessman-fence devotes the major part of his time and realises the vast majority of his income from his trade in stolen merchandise the amateur trade is done as a strictly on-the-side activity. Those who take part in the trade do not expect their illegal activities to earn them a living ... [and] the dealer gets little financial profit from his activity. Ultimately, his full-time hidden economy enterprise is always secondary to his full-time, legitimate job.

(Henry 1978: 20)

Although Del maintained receiving stolen property was a 'secondary' activity ('All my aspects of gain is always through work, it's not through how I've got bits and pieces'), it is difficult to see how in reality he could differentiate income gained from buying and selling stolen goods and his more legitimate activities, since both were integral and inseparable aspects of his life. He made no attempt to differentiate his income according to this criteria, and whatever the level of denial, his illegitimate operations, where a dozen regular thieves (in addition to the occasional passing thieves) visited the yard every week, must have been profitable.

Del evaded the more obvious exploitative role of receiving by emphasising that both his business and his customers were 'friends'. He said:

I think I make a friend of everybody, you know, they're not customers they're friends. Like to me if a customer comes more than three times they're a friend or a mate. It's not 'Please can I have?', it's 'Del have you got?' It's mainly first names ... the business is a friend and the customers that are coming are just friends of the business.

Del's comments are interesting for two reasons. First, despite operating in a 'shady' world, an element of trust was established. This is similar to Durkheim's (1964) notion that a moral order must underpin an economic contract. Second, Del readily admitted that dealing with friends was easier than dealing with strangers as they were 'more likely to see things your way'. 'I'm more likely to drop down a few quid for a stranger than I am a friend,' he said. So in fact we arrive back at Del's original description of himself as a businessman who, with exceptions such as family, did not let any opportunity to make money pass him by.

Although Del was known to the police as a dealer and thieves had actually been arrested in his yard, neither fact made him feel particularly insecure about his own position, because he took steps to ensure that the risk of prosecution was small. Del sometimes paid 'protection money' to certain police officers and occasionally supplied information (mostly drugs related). Supplying information did not result from any general identification with the police or their role, but rather from more moral concerns which many of the older generation shared about drug use and abuse (although at a practical level, this occasional informing probably gave Del a little bargaining power with the police.) The most important method Del employed to reduce the risk of detection, however, was dealing with known and trusted people. He argued:

> It'd have to be I know you, they know them attitude. I'd go to Barry, but I wouldn't necessarily go to Barry's mate. Barry'd have to go to Barry's mate, I'd go 'your kettle now Barry', because I know full well if Barry's picked a wrong'n then he's dealin' with it – it don't come back to me, it only goes as far as Barry. Everytime, it's a matter of protecting yourself... normally you find the thief that comes into a scrap yard has got a friend who's a thief, who's got a friend who's a thief and it tails from that.

Del describes below the kind of business he would undertake with anyone and, in pointing out the risks, illustrates his ingenuity and ability to use the language of the informal economy to talk himself out of situations where necessary.

> If someone came up to me, say this guy with the shoes. As far as that's concerned I'll deal with anybody, because even if you're being screwed [set up by the police] you're only gonna say 'yes' or 'no' in a pub. Now if you're being screwed you're not doing wrong you're just doin' business, you know it's as simple as that. It's only when the guy goes, 'I've got a pair of nicked shoes' and you go 'Oh I'll have 'em', then you're in trouble you're no longer doin' business, you know what you're doin'. If the guy goes 'Oh look I've got a pair of shoes for five quid, do you want 'em?' 'Yeah, I'll have 'em', but as soon as he says 'I've nicked 'em, they're five quid', then you're up against it, you know what you're about. It's a matter of how it comes across to me. You always know, no one would sell a pair of shoes for five quid, you know they're bent. The thing is unless you're told it's only in your mind and in the court I don't think that stands up does it, your own opinion of things? It's gotta be like actual facts, so what I think doesn't really matter. I can think oh the guy's nicked 'em but unless he tells me they're nicked, they're not nicked. So you work

from that really, you always know, but it's a chance you take. At the end of the day, you've gotta argue with the police about it. I think out of the things I've learned is how to answer the police.[4]

The presentation of a credible story is an important feature of delinquent accounts, as are the explanations which justify and neutralise behaviour. These will be discussed in greater depth both in this chapter and in later ones, but for the moment, I want to focus on Del's business, the kinds of goods he deals in, and how these are a consequence of opportunities presented by the scrap trade itself.

Henry's description of those who participate in amateur trading as 'ordinary people in [otherwise] honest jobs' would be difficult to reconcile with Del's occupation, stereotypically portrayed as villainous and on the fringes of semi-legitimate and illegitimate practices. Jimmy realistically commented, 'You've gotta be a bit of a rogue to do what he does for a living.' Hebdige confirms this viewpoint:

> criminal associations tend to cluster around certain jobs and the lines between fact and fiction, legality and law-breaking are even more confused in these cases.
>
> (Hebdige 1977:18)

Although Del's business acumen and manner were important in his level of entrepeneurial success, he was essentially no different from other scrap dealers in the area who also bought and sold stolen goods. He told me: 'in the scrap game you're gonna find a certain type of group thieving and skullduggery, you go down the market the same things happenin' but . . . with different items.'

Del bought a surprising variety of goods ranging from cars (and all related accessories) to video recorders, food, clothes, and drink. In an average week in the yard:

> I'd say . . . you'd get a good eight to ten people come in . . . with bent gear. . . and ask yer whether you want somethink or the other. . . . You'd normally find at least twice a week, someone'll come in and go 'I've got a mark four [Cortina] what parts do you want off it?', where they've gone and stolen the motor and got a nice set of wheels on it or wings or bonnet and then they'll go and strip off what you want, and fetch it back to yer; or 'I've got a box of tools, need any radios or batteries?' . . . Car radios, televisions come in quite often, stolen cars quite often, tools and things like that, a colossal amount of tools, CBs when they was in the rage.

You'll find that it's what's in the rage at the time, when videos first come out then you'd be flooded with videos. Radios, things like that, clothes come in ever such a lot, boxes of 'em. Gold comes in quite a lot, I mean necklaces, things like that but on trays, and a hell of a lot of drink comes through.

Del not only received goods but also sent regular thieves out with orders, especially if they had stolen cheque cards and credit cards.

Normally you'll find a guy comes into yer with his little box of tools that he's nicked and you're gonna give him his fiver. Before he goes he always says 'What do yer want?' and he'll go and get ...it. .... I had a guy not long ago he hadn't been out [of prison] two days and he was fetching Access cards to me and American Express. I send 'em out to get stuff, then I ain't buying stolen goods for a start.

A rapid turnover was also important as it reduced the likelihood of detection and minimised risk. Del therefore rarely bought goods without knowing where to sell them, and kept a mental note of who wanted what. He told me:

Normally I try and handle stuff that I know I can get rid of straight away. Clothing and things like that it's easy enough down the market... I've normally got to know where it's going. .... You never buy anythink unless you've got it sold – if someone comes in with car radios or anything like that, you'll sell 'em all day long – someone'll come in if you're givin' £5 or £10 for 'em and you'll get £15 or £20 for 'em. If you think you're gonna get stuck with 'em, sell 'em for a tenner, get yer money back.

Del's receiving role altered dramatically when he was forced to sell his scrap yard and move into a garage business. He lost much of his 'passing trade' and while many of his regular thieves continued to do business with him, he found that some thieves stopped coming because they felt he was becoming too successful. Del argued: 'It seems the more you get the less thieves trust yer.' I asked him if this was because they felt he was making too much money out of it. He replied:

Yeah probably. I mean why they get that attitude I've no idea. I've never thought about it. If I've sold somethink I've never thought oh well he's gonna go and make a fortune out of that. I've got what I wanted for it and that's all that matters and most of the people that I've dealt with have always been of that attitude. But I think when they see you gettin' too far, they think it beyond theirselves to come to yer and they'd rather go and find a littler Del, cos they're on equal terms as it were.

Del's comments illustrate the many grey areas which exist in the semi-legitimate and illegitimate world and that thieves and fences find their own level. They also indicate, however, that the traditional image of the exploitative receiver (cf Colquhoun 1800, Hall 1935, Chappell and Walsh 1974) may be an accurate one, but remains covert until there has been a visible display of changed financial circumstances. Del's assertion that those who came to him did so because he was reliable and trusted was clearly balanced with a certain image of his position and capital. When he was seen to extend his business interests, obviously assumed by thieves to be the fruits of his dealing, he became a bigger fish than they wished to deal with since he was no longer considered to be on the same level as them.

Del recognised at an abstract level that receiving was a crime and had an exploitative side to it. However, like Vince in Klockars's study, he argued that it wasn't hurting anybody and that if he didn't receive then someone else would. He told me:

I only receive because if I don't somebody else is gonna, so why shouldn't I make a profit? ... I always look [at it, that] out of everythink I do no one gets hurt in the end.

Klockars (1975) argues that such statements are both appealing and probably accurate, because if an individual fence stopped dealing others would simply fill the place. Nevertheless participants remain morally responsible for their actions, as Klockars eloquently states:

Responsibility for action is responsibility for action. Whether or not an act is likely to occur without one is simply irrelevant to the evaluation of one's own conduct. To surrender that elementary premise of simple moral philosophy is to abandon the responsibility to refuse to participate when one believes that others are doing wrong. Middle-class mothers everywhere, sensitive always to the seductions of the world, have correctly admonished their children who 'went along with the crowd': 'Just because everyone else jumps off the cliff doesn't mean you have to.' It is an admonition of considerable rhetorical sophistication which has absolutely nothing to do with jumping off of cliffs, but gets instantly to the heart of patently attractive denials of responsibility like 'If I don't buy it somebody else will.'

(Klockars 1975: 143)

Although Del recognised the criminal nature of his activity he did not see himself as a criminal or villain ('I don't think I've ever been a villain, I've been around a few villains but I've not been a villain') and talked about crime as something he used to be involved in during his teens and 20s rather than anything which accurately described his current activities. Yet when I asked him directly if he felt receiving was a crime, he told me:

It's a crime, in fact it's worse, it's the worse thing of all because without a receiver it's not worth stealing and nine times out of ten the receiver ends up with more of a profit margin than the thief.

Klockars believes these contradictions are easily explained in Vince's case because while he 'would accept that without receivers there would be no thieves, he did not feel this applied to him personally.' Hebdige's research in Fulham supports Del's arguments in the context of the scrap trade. He argues:

Despite three convictions for receiving stolen metal, the last conviction fetching a two month prison sentence, Sullivan was generally considered 'straight' or at least not overtly criminal and existed in that no man's land between legality and law breaking, which. . . appears to be quite densely populated in Fulham.

(Hebdige 1977: 26–7)

Despite the exploitative nature of the dealer's role in the exchange of stolen goods, Del maintained that some of his practices were based on 'moral' rather than business criteria. For example he argued that if people came into the yard and identified their property he altruistically gave it back!

I've actually bought stuff and the owners come in and I've just give it back to 'em. If they've found it then good luck to 'em, they can have it back – might have cost me ten, fifteen pound, doesn't matter, he's come in, 'OK, it's yours, have it.'

Del also argued that he would not deal with 'mugging-type thieves' and those involved in drugs.

I've never dealt with the mugging-type thieves, I've never had

anything to do with them cos I think I'd bash 'em on the head.
Mine are more property-type thieves as it were, the cars, the handbags, or whatever. Just people with no money, it's easy money for
'em.

Although these practices added weight to Del's assertion that he did not
harm anyone, in reality it was very difficult to maintain, since people
who stole handbags could be muggers, and drug addicts steal car radios
to support their habits. It is likely that not dealing with 'mugging-type
thieves' was reduced to colour rather than any other criteria, as mugging
was regarded as a 'black' crime. However such beliefs formed part of
the techniques of neutralization (Sykes and Matza 1957) which offered
rationalizations and explanations for behaviour and enabled these
practices to take place. It is to these issues which I now turn.

The normality of crime: attitudes, thoughts, and rationalisations

The ease with which business was conducted among Del and the other
clientele in the Grafton was influenced by their attitudes towards crime
and deviant behaviour in general. 'Doin' business' and buying stolen
goods was not considered to be a crime at all, while the terms which
were used to refer to it, like 'getting a bargain or something on the
cheap', neutralized and rationalized the criminal nature of the act, and
provided the necessary explanations for such acts to take place (cf Mills
1940). Several sorts of rationalisations were adopted, as the following
discussion reveals.

The first set of rationalizations regulars employed focused on the
proposition that given the opportunity anyone would buy 'cheap' goods
and therefore they should not be held personally culpable. As Chris
argued:

> If someone came up and offered me a suede coat for £20 and it
> fitted, I wouldn't ask no questions, I'd take it. But then most
> people are like that, aren't they.

Joanne said:

> I think we all do it sooner or later. We all know they're stolen
> although you might not have stole 'em, we all know. I've had 'em,
> they've been cheap, like if someone offers you a cheap washing
> machine and you knew it was stolen, well it must be stolen for a
> brand new washing machine say for a hundred pound or a video,

you're not gonna ask no questions, you're gonna buy it because it's cheap and I think that's how everyone thinks. Even me mum and dad would have it.

Regulars often pointed to the normality of 'doin' business' because even their parents did it. Jimmy, for example, described his father as 'whiter than white', but proceeded later in an interview to detail his hidden economy activities.

I don't think me dad knows how to spell the word trouble let alone bleedin' what's in it. Although don't get me wrong: since me dad's been older I've learned a few things that make him not so bleedin' innocent – 300 gallons of paint a week [taken from work], it ain't no mean feat, by any stretch of the imagination.

Sykes and Matza's (1957) 'techniques of neutralization' offer a way of understanding the seeming contradiction that although deviants realise certain behaviour is wrong, they still participate in it. This is because norms which are generally recognised and shared by delinquents themselves are 'suspended' during deviant acts. As delinquents realise their actions are 'wrong' they require a number of justifications to explain their behaviour.

Everyone's at it

They're on the take for whatever they can get without a shadow of a doubt. We'll go through the duty frees at London airport with an extra bottle of scotch and another 200 fags but they don't go through customs cos they've got their own boats, pop across to France to buy a few of these and earn a few quid on 'em. No they're on the take: it's just on a bigger scale. There is not anybody in this country with the exception say of the Queen that is not on the take.

(Jimmy)

In some ways a rather conspiratorial world view was adopted by those in the Grafton, where the belief that everyone was 'at it' applied equally to those in positions of power and privilege, who were in fact seen to be 'at it' more than most. These 'moral hypocrites' (Henry 1978) such as police, judges, and magistrates formed one of the most important justifications for behaviour. As Matza (1964) argued, the '"accused" directed criticism at the accusers', questioning their legitimacy and competence as a way of detracting attention from their own deviant actions.

If officials are extremly ineffective, could it not perhaps be that *everybody commits many offences* and only a few suffer the misfortune of apprehension? . . . Once apprehended, official cognizance is focused and the chances of subsequent apprehension maximized. This possibility . . . is the darkest suspicion of subcultural delinquency and the most profound basis for its sense of injustice.

(Matza 1964: 149, original emphasis)

Although attitudes towards the police and other criminal justice agencies will be discussed in later chapters, in the context of this discussion it is interesting to see how the adults' generally negative attitudes towards the police were reinforced by personal experiences other than those from official contacts or the media. Some time before the fieldwork began, two police officers (Alex and Joe) played in the men's darts team and 'did' business like any of the other regulars. This clearly influenced already prejudicial attitudes and became a justification in itself. Jimmy, for example, said of the police:

I know they're bigger fuckin' rogues than I am. It's as simple as that – Alex is. I was taken back first off when I found he was a copper. I thought I'll steer clear of him, but then you get to know him. . . anythink that I had he'd buy so that he could sell his gear at . . . police station. Anythink honestly, we've been to dart matches before and all our team has had the same shirts on – truck loads went missing. I've had it, bleedin' Alex has had 'em, we've all had 'em. You can't tell me that they're not bleedin' rogues.

Del argued that although he was always suspicious in Alex's company, he exhibited many of the same attitudes:

I was always wary. If you was in a conversation Alex's ear'oles are sort of goin' and I s'ppose I'm wary cos if you're talkin' criminal, you don't want the coppers. But if he did 'wig in' nine times out of ten he'd come in on the conversation and quite agree with it.

Del and his contemporaries did not condemn the powerful and privileged for exploiting their situation (because if they had been fortunate enough to swap places they assumed they would behave in the same way) but resented the different treatment they received if apprehended.

As Del commented, 'There's two laws: a law for the law and a law for the others, there always will be, can't alter that.' While Jimmy said:

All right so I'm not sayin' that if I was to become an MP that I wouldn't abuse it. All depends what you could get away with. But as I say on a larger scale. I get away with a lot but on a lot smaller scale. . . . All right they get away with it, what people don't know won't hurt 'em. But when they get caught they get treated differently to anybody else, not worse, cos all they've gotta do is resign from the force, but they're fuckin' free.

Jimmy's comment, 'what people don't know won't hurt 'em', again emphasises the distinction between public knowledge and private practice. As long as activities remain covert and are not subjected to the rule of law or negative sanction they are quite acceptable. Therefore there was nothing wrong with crime as long as you don't get caught. Matza (1964) suggests that delinquents can maintain this viewpoint by adopting a 'juristic' view of crime where statements such as 'No, I never commited a crime like that – I mean to say I never got caught doing that' are not viewed as contradictory. Simply because the informal economy operates largely unhindered by contacts with the criminal justice system within groups and communities which positively sanction such behaviour, people rarely have to confront the moral proposition that stealing is wrong. Joanne, for example, argued:

It's wrong but then I do it. The way I look at it, I didn't steal it so I'm not worried about it. I suppose it would be a different story if I got found out and the police done me for accepting stolen property.

Another way to justify activities which carry some moral stigma is to adopt the attitude that certain forms of behaviour can be excused if they are compared with other, perhaps worse, behaviour. This is particularly prevalent when comparing crimes against property and crimes against the person and is a particularly popular explanation for white-collar crime (cf Sutherland 1949, Cressey 1953). Levens (1964) for example argued that white-collar criminals 'did not conceive of themselves as criminals. This epithet still conveyed to them, as to most people, the image of the thug, the bank robber, the demoniacal and notorious villain who clubs old ladies in dark alleys.'

Once it is established that some forms of crime are worse than others, those participating in lesser behaviour are excused guilt. Take the attitudes of Joanne and Chris, for example. Joanne complained that during a day trip to Southend, the police stopped Billy in his car:

> They was just silly things like no tax disc mainly. But he kept on gettin' pulled for the same old thing. I don't know what it was, either laziness for not buyin' it or some't wrong, defective tyre, somethink like that. Once they pull yer up they go right over the car, he got pulled up cos he got no tax disc then they nicked him for that and cos his horn didn't work. We was at Southend, we had Michelle with us goin' there for the day. I'd just gone and got the fish and chips and they come out and they stopped him and they know you're out for the day, it's just somethink so minor whereas up the road someone's probably gettin' mugged.

Joanne felt personally victimised by this incident, arguing that the police had deliberately 'picked on them' as they 'knew' she and Billy were out for the day. Her explanation of events allowed her to direct criticism at the police rather than Billy himself, arguing that they should have been dealing with the 'real criminals', instead of 'silly things' resulting from Billy's 'laziness'. Chris used similar techniques to minimise Del's adult activities because they were not as serious as those he was involved in as a youth (see Chapter 3). The denial of a victim was also an important and pervasive justification, particularly in cases of crime against property (cf Horning 1970). Del, for example, described credit card fraud as the 'perfect crime' because 'no one but the banks lost out'.

> Kitin', cheques. I thought that was dead classic. I mean who's gonna lose? The banks. That is when it goes further than yer own. The bank is not yer own, the bank is infinity, it's nobody, there's no one really gonna lose out of it.

Thieving off the rich

One of the most popular justifications about crime among the adult generation was that the codes thieves employed ensured they were only stealing from people who could afford it! Barry, for example, argued: 'There's a system that thieves always have that you never thieve off yer own, they only do people who can afford to lose it.' While Chris argued: 'I s'ppose the fact that he's robbin' from the people who always had lots of money anyway and claimed it back off the insurance, that wasn't so bad as if he was going out and really doin' somethink.'

As other commentators have noted (Henry 1978, Ditton 1977, Read 1984) such attitudes are not the result of advanced levels of class consciousness and are rarely realised in practice. Chris's comments above serve as an example. First, she suspends her own experience of having been a victim of crime and knew, despite being insured, that it was the sentimental rather than the actual value of the goods she lost which most disturbed her. Second, many victims in working-class districts are not insured (since on most of the local estates it was virtually impossible to get insurance) but Del bought and sold their property and made a profit from it. Third, it is doubtful that most of the property he dealt with came from rich people anyway (since there were very few affluent people in the area) and most of the thieves who visited the yard operated locally. It is therefore 'their own' whose homes were generally unguarded and uninsured that were most likely to be victims.

Del was more realistic in his estimation of the code:

> I don't particularly like the idea of people saying I don't steal off me own; I only steal off the rich. I could be the classic example seven years ago I didn't have two bob, people'd steal off me now. I'm still one of 'em. In fact I'm as much one of 'em now as I've ever been. So I don't believe that I won't steal off me own cos everybody's yer own, the only ones that aren't yer own are the ones that are born with silver spoons.

Del provided an example which illustrates how the code could be contravened but also points to ways in which a certain 'honour amongst thieves' does operate.

Del: I got nicked for a drivin' offence in one of [my employer's] vans. He said he'd always pay the fine whatever else, cos it was a dog of a van. I wound up with £100 fine, and he knocked me [didn't pay up]. . . . I was talkin' to Barry about it and he goes 'We'll go down and get it'. So we went down and broke into his house. Now all I'm concerned about is I want my £100, that's all I want. . . . But Barry wants to clear the house out, and Barry did. I didn't have any satisfaction out of doin' that – the only satisfaction I had was gettin' my £100. I don't think that was very criminal, I felt I was doing justice.

JF: Do you think what Barry did was criminal ?

Del: Yeah. Cos I was stealin' off me own! . . . If the guy
            hadn't said an iota to me, if he had said 'You drive it,
            then you're on yer own' that would have suited me cos
            I knew what the thing was. But as soon as he said 'If
            you get a fine I'll pay it' then he's made his bed, and
            he's got to honour his word to me.

The normality of crime and getting caught

The preceding discussion has illustrated that by a variety of mechanisms
crime was positively sanctioned and formed an institutionalised,
unquestioned practice in an environment where it appeared that
everyone was 'at it'. The literature often assumes that these practices
would be less persistent if the likelihood of getting caught were greater
(cf Becker 1970) and that once apprehended, offenders are easily
deterred (cf Cameron 1964). This view is premised on a belief that
hidden economy exploits result from calculated and well-thought-out
plans where participants assess the likelihood of getting caught. If the
risks are small then people will take them; if they are high they will not
(cf Becker 1970). However, as Del argues, questions of rationality and
the likelihood of getting caught only come after the event.

> You never think about it before you do it. You don't think I might
> not get away with it, it's only when they've got yer in their hand
> you think they've got me. . . . You don't think police while you're
> thinkin' steal. The two don't go. I think I've always had this thing
> where I've known whether I'm gonna get caught or not gonna get
> caught. You know when you're doin' it, you know full well that
> you're gonna go in there and you're gonna get caught and sod me
> you still go and do it! There's somethink tellin' yer you're gonna
> get caught this time. You could have been to the same place five,
> ten times and know full well you're gonna walk in and out, and
> one day you walk in and think it's gonna happen today and it
> would.

What is lacking in accounts of hidden economy trading is the history of
the participants, how they joined the network, the nature of previous
criminal involvement, how networks are formed and maintained. Seen
in a wider context, such practices and the sanctioning of them are part of
a complex grey area of deviant activities, perpetrated by adults who
have previous careers and experiences of criminal justice agencies,

living in a community 'with an excess of definitions favourable to violation of laws' (Sutherland 1949). Although getting caught has important consequences, most notably in teaching people how not to get caught again, it did not, for those described here at least, bring about desistance.

Unlike the middle-class world, where trouble with the police may invite censure and stigma, for many of the residents of Gorer Lane and Stanton this was simply not the case. As I illustrated in Chapter 1, many people in the area were involved in some kind of shady business and although they may have recognised that their activities were wrong at an abstract level, this did not prevent them from engaging in them. Essentially, a different set of values pertained where certain kinds of crime were not regarded as wrong. When I asked Del, for example, if he had any regrets he replied, 'No. The only thing I've done wrong is get caught, that's all.' Crime is normal and 'gettin' caught' is the catch. There is no reason to believe that successive brushes with authority will change such a view; in fact with each subsequent contact it may harden and reinforce it. Whilst people say that getting caught or being incarcerated has made a difference and changed their behaviour (arguing that they have a greater sense of worth and take fewer risks) their behaviour does not always bear this out. What does change, however, is their ability to present a more adequate and convincing public self. Szasz (1973) was undoubtedly correct in his estimation that 'men are often more interested in better justifying themselves than behaving themselves'. Faced with official sanctions and having been labelled deviant, the offender must explain his behaviour in a language which his listener can understand. How many times do offenders at this stage say 'I won't do it again' and then leave the court and within hours, weeks, or months returns to the same activities. They continue because essentially they do not undergo any change in attitude at all. It is to a detailed account of the formation and development of these attitudes which I now turn in Chapter 3.

Summary

This chapter has described the adult generation who socialised in the Grafton Arms public house and the business which was conducted among regulars there. I argued that previous accounts of hidden economy trading are often discussed in a cultural vacuum, and that participants' past offending, the way in which networks are formed, and wider social and cultural factors often receive little attention. Nevertheless the persistence and success of business networks depends on the presence of numerous rationalisations and explanations for behaviour which minimise the proposition that either stealing or receiving stolen goods is 'wrong'.

Notes

1   There were a number of people who frequented the Grafton with whom I had little or no contact. One young man sat in the public bar, but no one ever spoke to him. There were also 'floaters' - people who used the pub a couple of nights a week, perhaps on Friday nights, or occasionally on their way home from work. However, it was the clique who were the most established group and who invested both a great deal of time (and money!) in the pub.

2   I made what enquiries I could to confirm this information and the claim may not be as outlandish as it appears. Hebdige (1977: 18) noted in his study of Fulham that 'The mini-cab firms in South London are notorious for their sharp practices and rivalries tend to escalate into open warfare (petrol bombs etc). Ben, who has been a driver for a local mini-cab firm, told me that within a week of working there he had been given the phone number of a "heavy" who lived in South London. If he required this man's services he could get them at a specially reduced rate. He claimed he could have shot someone in the legs for as little as £20. There was enough support for these activities in Harry's case that I decided not to pursue taped interviews with him.

3   On evenings when there were no darts matches Del would regularly be involved in business, although this did not appear to be his primary motivation for being in the pub, as he played darts and scored games with everyone else. On occasions where he anticipated or had arranged to do more serious business Del left his darts at home.

4   Del was not correct about the laws of receiving, since the Theft Act (1968: sec.22), states:

> A person handles stolen goods if (otherwise than in the course of stealing) knowing or believing them to be stolen goods he dishonestly receives the goods, or dishonestly undertakes or assists in their retention, removal, disposal or realisation by or for the benefit of another person, or if he arranges to do so.

Chapter three

Tracing the steps: the evolution of attitudes

all causes [of delinquency] do not operate at the same time, and we need a model which takes into account the fact that patterns of behaviour develop in orderly sequence . . . we must deal with a sequence of steps, of changes in the individual's behaviour and perspectives, in order to understand the phenomenon.

(Becker 1963: 23)

The previous chapter described the primary couples who frequented the Grafton Arms, the business which was conducted there, and the attitudes of the clientele towards such activities. I emphasized that the cultural context is crucial to the formation of attitudes and 'business' networks. This chapter traces the development of attitudes from youth to adulthood, through the histories of Del, Jimmy, and Barry: their experiences of the education system, initial contacts with the police and other criminal justice agencies, the extent and nature of their activities, and how they moved from the highly visible public sphere of juvenile crime, to the more private and institutionalised sphere which replaced it at adulthood.

These three case studies are in no way meant to support a generalised theory, but the men's experiences find ample support in other accounts of British working-class culture (Downes 1966, Willis 1977, Willmott 1966, Mays 1954, Patrick 1973, Parker 1974). Furthermore, although obviously impressionistic, my observations of the police supported my view that Del, Jimmy, and Barry were typical of many people in South London with whom the police came into contact.

A great deal of research has focused on identifying factors which are conducive to the development of delinquency. One of the most thorough longitudinal research studies in this area was conducted by West and his colleagues at the Institute of Criminology at Cambridge. Based on criminal records and interview data collected over an extended period of time, the team highlighted the importance of family background, anti-authoritarian attitudes, educational experience, and anti-social behaviour in delinquency. They suggested that 'many of the hard core of recidivist delinquents . . . had been recognizably deviant from an early age, living in unhappy homes at eight, noticeably troublesome at school at age ten and reported by teachers to be aggressive in their behaviour at age twelve' (West and Farrington 1977: 160). Table 4 illustrates the social characteristics which the Cambridge researchers identified between the delinquent and non-delinquent groups. The initials B, J, and D indicate similar experiences or characteristics in Barry, Del, and Jimmy.

Table 4 Contrasts between delinquents and non-delinquents on eleven social characteristics

	Social characteristic	Total men concerned	% among 101 delinquents	% among 228 non-delinquents
B	Tattooed	35	22.8	4.17
	High on self-reported aggression	79	45.5	11.5
BJD	Unstable job record	92	45.5	16.0
BJD	Spends leisure 'hanging about'	42	21.8	7.0
BJD	Involved in anti-social groups	81	37.6	14.9
BJD	Admits drinking and driving	85	38.6	16.0
(?)	Heavy gambler	87	37.6	17.0
BJD	Sexually experienced	164	69.3	32.6
BD	Heavy smoker	104	43.6	20.8
B	Has used prohibited drugs	122	48.5	25.3
BJD	Anti-establishment attitudes	98	36.6	21.2

Source: West 1982: 62

Although Del and his contemporaries experienced many of the common indices thought to be conducive to delinquency (they grew up in low-income areas in difficult family circumstances) these factors do not necessarily provide the most valuable method of charting their delinquent careers, because such individual explanations exclude the importance of the traditions of crime and delinquency present in the area and the local opportunity structures which existed for Del and his friends during their youth. They exploited these structures because of their knowledge of the local networks and cultural inheritance of attitudes which emphasised the pursuit of easy money, a valued and rational activity for youths and adults alike. As Mays (1954) argued, delinquency in the inner city is 'not so much a symptom of maladjustment as of adjustment to a sub-culture in conflict with the culture of the city as a whole.'

Hopping the wag: the attitude to school

If you're gonna learn somethink you've gotta enjoy it and I never enjoyed school at all. Nobody ever taught me to enjoy school, they just said 'you will learn' and that was it. Then you went and done what you wanted to do and the more I could hop the wag the better I was.

(Barry)

A great deal of research has focused on the relationship between educational experience and delinquency (Douglas 1964, Douglas *et al.* 1968, Goldthorpe *et al.* 1969, Hargreaves 1967, Willis 1977) because successive generations of working-class youths have often found the streets more exciting than the classroom, where formal learning is viewed as boring and difficult to adjust to, both linguistically (cf Bernstein 1959, Labov 1972) and in terms of discipline. The links between truancy and delinquency are also well established (May 1975, Douglas *et al.* 1968, Tennett 1971, West and Farrington 1977).

Del, Jimmy, and Barry all experienced considerable problems in the school environment from the outset and their anti-authoritarian attitudes were already quite pronounced in primary school years. Barry, for example, found it virtually impossible to adapt to the discipline of school and told me: 'I was always trouble – I was always fighting, . . . all the way through, . . . primary school right the way through secondary school.' As the classroom held little interest or value, all three began the habit of 'hoppin' the wag' (truanting from school), which they saw as the beginning of their street experience. Barry told me:

O levels and stuff like that was not my idea of fun, I was never one for school, I just wasn't interested so therefore you find an outlet and the outlet was 'hop the wag'. You dive around and that's when you start gettin' into trouble, different items you know. You're on the street all day, you want money, so with us it was the old telephone boxes to start off with, then from there it went on to cars and different other items.

Whilst Del argued

> It all stems back to hoppin' the wag, ... you only know it afterwards, you don't know it then, but this is the time you're gonna get yerself in a bind.

Willis (1977) argues that the education system prepares working-class youths for a life of 'labour' and suggests that counter-school cultures anticipate the shop-floor culture for which many are destined. For Del and his contemporaries, generational continuity was not derived from shop-floor culture but the autonomy of self-employment and entrepeneurial 'duckin' and divin'' which was a prevalent feature of the area. By early adolescence the 'focal concerns' of 'trouble, toughness, smartness, excitement, fate and autonomy', described by Miller (1958) as central to those of the lower classes, were all apparent.

Street life and the pursuit of easy money

Crime and delinquency research since Cohen's (1955) pioneering work in the 1950s has debated whether delinquency is an extension of lower-class values (Miller 1958, Downes 1966) or a rejection or inversion of them (Cohen 1955, Cloward and Ohlin 1960), whether there is a culture of delinquency or a delinquent subculture (Matza 1964). However, the recurring theme in all such studies is the emphasis on delinquency as a 'collective solution' (Cohen 1955, Brake 1973, 1980, 1985) to problems of masculine identity where the peer group plays a vital role.

Many of the activities in which Del and his contemporaries were engaged during their teens were very similar to those of the present-day youths and involved acts of vandalism, breaking and entering, fighting, and stealing from cars (although they did not involve 'taking and driving away', which was prevalent in the older of the two contemporary youth groups.) From 9 or 10 years of age until their mid-teens, the street, old bombsites, and disused canal provided playgrounds for Del and his friends, and it was during this period that they went in search of excitement, developed a 'street-wise' identity, and experienced their initial contacts with law-enforcement agencies.

'Hopping the wag' created the need to fill time and obtain money and it was this instrumental orientation which emerged in the earliest accounts of juvenile crime. Any opportunity which afforded itself was exploited to the full, as Del describes in some of his first misdeamenours:

I s'ppose it was walking around, you start smoking, that's where the problems really start cos you can't get the money for the fags. 'Hopping the wag' with someone else, [you] go along and see a radio in a car, you think oh I could get a couple of quid for that radio. . . . The very first time I went to court, nicking a bottle of lemonade. Very clever that was, we done the shop along from the school. It used to have an alley way beside it and he used to put his bottles in the back, which we used to take and give them to him at the front [in the shop] for the threepence or whatever it was on the bottle. It took him a hell of a lot of time to suss it out. It just happened that one day while I was at the back gettin' the bottles to take to the front, the police were sittin' there waiting for me.

Mayer (1980) argued that the need for 'easy money' was the primary motivation for juvenile offending. While Parker's (1974) account of the 'Catseye business' (stealing car radios) emphasised that this was a rational activity for economic ends. Although financial rewards might be irregular and small, the pursuit of 'easy money' could in some circumstances become a lucrative enterprise. For example Jimmy at 15 operated a successful 'business' stealing scooters and selling the parts:

We used to go out at night . . . wherever we see one that we'd like, take it, break it down in the flats, keep 'em there and sell the parts. I got known as somebody who fixed scooters. We used to do that quite a lot to earn ourselves money until I got caught and put inside. . . . It bought me a regular income.

This entrepeneurial spirit was also reflected in the adolescent generation (see Chapter 5) and is an important constituent in the transition from the public juvenile experience to the private hidden economy exploits in later years.

Early experience of police and courts

Authority officials are not seen as exercising 'authority' but 'power' and 'might'. They are seen as unfair and unjust.

(Parker 1974: 185)

Although prevailing cultural factors were important in the development of attitudes and activities among both youths and adults, it was not simply a matter of direct 'cultural determinism'. Adolescence and the sense of rebellion which it encompassed left each subsequent generation the opportunity for independent experience, which in turn tended to confirm those of the parent generation. Liebow's observations of the Negro community in Washington are particularly apt in this regard. He argued:

> many similarities between the lower-class Negro father and son (or mother and daughter) do not result from 'cultural transmission', but from the fact that the son goes out and independently experiences the same failures, in the same areas, and for much the same reasons as his father. What appears as a dynamic, self-sustaining cultural process is, in part at least, a relatively simple piece of social machinery which turns out, in rather mechanical fashion, independently produced look alikes.
>
> (Liebow 1967: 223)

Although both generations expressed similar attitudes towards law-enforcement agencies (a sense of injustice at malpractice, the desire to score a success and get one over on 'Old Bill'), early recollections of the police before any overt contact took place on the streets did not contain such elements, rather they encapsulated a 'Dixon of DockGreen' image. Although Del and his contemporaries later realised the extent of their parents' hostile and antagonistic attitudes towards the police, these did not appear to affect their own perceptions before they had experienced contacts with the police themselves.

Perhaps because of the time dimension in looking back to adolescence, and a predisposition to see the past in more romanticised terms (cf Pearson, G. 1983), much of the fiery injustice expressed in the present-day youths (see Chapter 5) had subsided, and it was common amongst the people in this generation to speak of the 'old-type coppers' of their youth who appeared to have more time for young people and acted as a greater deterrent. Del for example argued:

> You always found that the police had more time for you, they wanted to know. I think the police were more of a frightener, more of a deterrent for younger kids. Cos I remember how the coppers would get hold of yer by the hand and that. They'd never sort of threaten yer with prison or threaten to take yer to yer mum, you'd get threatened with a backhander, wallop round the back of the head and you knew why you had the backhander. I s'ppose that's the impression of how I always felt about 'em.

Barry argued that although the police gave the appearance of keeping the peace, any influence they had on behaviour was transitory:

> People started ringing up the police [they'd] come round three or four times a week. Nine out of ten times it was always local police and they knew the area and they knew the locals and whether I was involved or not they used to come over, 'You're number one in the wagon', slapped yer hand, told yer off and let yer go. They had done their thing, someone had phoned up, they'd come round, people has seen 'em come round, they'd pulled somebody in. The people who'd phoned up were happy, the Old Bill's happy and I had a go, simple as that.

In the years between 10 and 15, Del, Jimmy, and Barry most often recollected incidents when they had got caught by the police. This was probably because such incidents were influential in formulating attitudes, and were crucial to learning the rudimentary rules of 'playing the game'. Barry recollects his earliest memories of the police:

> We was fighting at the top end of the street and the police came round, they had the old Black Marias then and they whacked us in the back, you know just talkin' and puttin' things over saying 'You could go in prison' and all this tryin' to frighten the hell out of yer really, but you get out of the waggon and you laugh at 'em. They're 'I'm the copper' ... – that was their status. They said 'Jump', we jumped but when they turned their backs people just laughed at 'em.

The seemingly cavalier attitude expressed by Barry masks an important element in experiences and attitudes towards law-enforcement agencies by all the generations. In relating encounters after the event they were often expressed without any mention of the fear with which they were actually experienced (cf Blagg 1985). Such descriptions served to perpetuate an image of toughness and an undeterred spirit. However, it was in these initial contacts with law-enforcement agencies that fear was most marked, because youngsters did not understand how the system operated. Del's description illustrates this:

> It wasn't the court that frightened me it was the station. . . . When you get that first thing where the police take yer into the 'peters' [cells] it's all right up until that point, don't matter you've been nicked, don't matter what's gonna come that first thing when they

go CRASH, and the doors gone and you're on yer own, that's when the old heart starts goin' boom, boom, boom. What's gonna happen now, what's me mum gonna say, is she gonna thrash me round the head, which they did often, well not me mum, usually me dad. I'd say it was a frightening experience that first time being banged up, you just don't know what's gonna happen, from the second time you're aware you know what's gonna happen, you know someone's gonna come and get yer out, you don't know how long but you know someone's gonna come in the end.

Reactions to police and courts

The more immediate, and sometimes violent, physical approach of the police ('talking to them in a language, they can understand') was viewed as much more real and threatening than the formalised ritual of the court. While the courts had the powers to enforce custodial sentences, the atmosphere, language and attitude of magistrates, judges, and the court administration were so far removed from the offenders' own experiences that the system and the rules which emanated from it were ridiculed (cf Carlen 1976). This was particularly true of the juvenile court, where the paternalistic approach of magistrates had little meaning to the street-wise youths' notions of the way they should have been dealt with. Del's description of his first court appearance at 13 for breaking and entering illustrates this:

> We'd hopped the wag from school and went up the old block of flats, got the old dinner knife which we've stolen from the school and tried to get this door open. I've gone with the knife, opened the door and the woman's grabbed hold of me. When we got to court it was like being taken to the headmaster. I was never frightened of it, they [magistrates] all seemed so sympathe'ic. I dunno whether it was the fact that it was my first time or what, they seemed too soft. I got a conditional discharge. I know it sounds stupid, but you automatically thought 'cooh, that was a piece of piss', you know, 'what was all that about, what a waste of time, I'd had worse off me dad before I got here.'

Barry was caught for armed robbery at 16, when he and a friend attempted to hold up a milkman, but successive court appearances had little impact on him. When I asked him what it was like being in court, he told me:

Great. It was the funniest time I've ever had. There used to be a geezer up there called Rubber Lips, he had a big pair of lips. If you went to court everyone knew Rubber Lips and his favourite trick was 'You've been a naughty boy so I'm gonna put you on probation and you will go and see your probation officer twice a week.' And you used to laugh at it cos the man was such an idiot, it was unbelievable. You look all dead serious and say 'Yeah' and you walk out of the court and shrug yer shoulders.

Barry's comments require further examination. His ridicule of the system was real enough, but his statement that his court appearance was the 'funniest time I ever had' was almost certainly 'ex-post facto' bravado.

Jimmy was remanded in custody at 15 for stealing scooters and, although put on probation after his court case, felt that the cost of having been publicly labelled 'deviant' changed people's attitudes towards him.

Oh they changed, everybody used to come round then saying 'Why did you do it, why did you do that?' You can never say I done that because of. . .

One might suspect from Jimmy's comment that this negative feedback influenced his behaviour. However, he also described how he played on the tough image of the borstal boy in school – 'watch out you know where I've just come out of' – and was to continue his visits to court throughout his 20s and into his 30s.

In this ten to fifteen-year period then, the lives of Jimmy, Del, and Barry were marked by absence from school, and juvenile crime of various kinds. Del, like Jimmy, was remanded in custody for burglary, and Barry was given a six-month Detention Centre sentence for burglary and armed robbery. Early contacts with criminal justice agencies did little to deter them but laid the foundations for injustices (cf Matza 1964), introduced them to the initial elements of 'playing the game', and encompassed important rationalisations about the reasons for their behaviour which will be discussed below.

Reflections on juvenile pasts

I got slung out of school when I was 14 so they stuck me in the sea cadets. I got slung out of there for fightin' too many times and it was just back on the streets really, and that's when you start gettin' involved with different sorts of people. It's just that sort of to be one of the lads you have got to sort of go with what they're doin' and that's when you end up gettin' in trouble.

(Barry)

The influence of the peer group, which sanctioned and supported the commission of anti-social acts, was the most frequent explanation given for juvenile behaviour. Integral to such arguments were observations that they were only doing what everyone else did (cf Willmott 1966); that they were led on by the crowd and to be 'one of the lads' *had* to be involved, and most of all a denial of responsibility for their actions. Barry argued: 'I mean I wasn't a nasty villain, I didn't go lookin' for it, it just used to find me, I don't know why it just did.' Parker (1976: 39) argues that trouble 'is not something you have to look for, but something you find yourself in'. Matza termed these explanations 'justification through apology'.

slogans of justification include, 'No one gives you anything. Take what you can get' . . . 'I had to join the gang and use a knife. A guy has to defend himself don't he?' His very slogans reveal his assessment of delinquency. It is necessary or unavoidable, but he evaluates it in terms of ordinary conventions. He excuses himself, but his gruff manner has obscured the fundamental sense in which he begs our pardon.

(Matza 1964: 42).

Matza argues that although delinquents are drawn towards crime they fully appreciate that this behaviour is wrong. As a result offenders must find explanations for their actions (what I have termed the formation of a credible story: see Chapters 2, 5, and 6). These accounts were often tailored to the expectation of a particular listener (see Chapter 6) and made explanations like being dragged along with the crowd very useful. Del, for example, argued that although there was much less likelihood of getting into trouble alone, 'being easily led' was a convenient but not necessarily accurate reflection of his role:

I've always been lucky in the respect that everyone that I've got into trouble with it's always their fault! You know what I mean, I'm easily led, everyone always said. I always used to accept that, that's good, yeah I'm easily led, yeah I'll have a bit of that. I think that what they didn't really realise was that I was the leader for the majority of it, but if it came to being captured mate, then yeah it was their fault, I didn't mind.[1]

Del, Jimmy, and Barry felt that it was important to differentiate between their juvenile pursuits, which were often motivated by 'devilment' and their activities in later years. Del, for example, argued:

It all seemed to happen in two years – all the sort of skullduggery as it were. It was just silly, it's not childish, it's a way of gettin' pennies easier I s'ppose. Cos kids of the age between 12 and 15 they don't wanna hurt anybody, . . . it's devilment. . . more than anythink but as I say even if it's devilment you've gotta be frightened out of it at an early age – otherwise [you] get stuck in it.

In the light of this undeterred 'devilment', Del, Jimmy, and Barry felt that law-enforcement agencies should actively deter crime. They all argued that someone should have intervened forcibly to prevent their behaviour and by failing to do so, criminal justice agencies were ineffectual, soft, and offered no deterrent. Although the threat, or experience, of actual violence was often seen to be the only effective means of deterring crime, when faced with such violence the outcome differed little from that of the courts. Del provides an excellent example of this when he was caught stealing lead by the owner of a scrap yard:

I'll tell yer that put the fear of God up me twice as much as any police could for a deterrent against it, they frightened seven shades of shit out of me. . . . The majority of it was threat but they did put us in a baler. I still say that I would have been six foot if I hadn't been put in that baler! . . . You thought you were dead, you wished to Christ you had never touched it, you did literally wish and all of a sudden there's a God and you want to meet him and you want him to help yer. I feel that if the courts had the power to do that, then certainly it would stop a lot of it.

One might conclude that Del, as a result of this experience, was sufficiently deterred to avoid venturing into scrap yards again. Whilst this experience undoubtedly had a lasting impact on him, it did little to change his behaviour. He was still stealing from yards and building sites in his mid-20s.

This notion of a strong deterrent was also reflected in another rationalisation about temptation, where crime was considered to be so easy that they *had* to do it. Like Hobbes's notion of man's innate selfish instincts and Durkheim's belief of the need to restrain man and his desires in order to achieve happiness, the role of temptation and the stupidity of those who owned property and did not protect it were both viewed as sanctioning crime. Del argued, 'There's temptation and temptation. It's too easy you've gotta do it.' Whilst Chris argued, 'There should be a way that it shouldn't be so easy for people to do it.'

The intermediate years

the approach of adulthood converts the possibility of public evaluation of delinquency to a probability. In the majority of cases, pairs of delinquents discover one after the other that they had shared misunderstandings. They had not really been committed to delinquency – it was fun and each thought that the others demanded it, but *they* had never really believed in it. However, this does not always happen. A very small proportion may discover that they are in fact committed to their misdeeds. These decide to be criminals.

(Matza 1964: 55–6, original emphasis)

Although it would be wrong to deny that there are important changes in juvenile and adult status which influence the commission of crimes, Matza's typology is over-simplistic. It excludes the multifaceted 'grey areas' between the legitimate world and that of professional crime, and suggests that most delinquents as they move into the adult world undergo a transformation in attitude. It will be argued here that far from changing, attitudes and behaviour simply progress and build upon the experience of youth.

Matza argues that one of the characteristics of juvenile delinquency is its episodic nature, which allows the individual to construct an image of self, neutralising behaviour which he knows to be wrong. This applies as much to adults as to adolescents who seek to negotiate an existence and exploit opportunities which present themselves, legitimate or otherwise. All the techniques of neutralisation so carefully fostered during youth, establishing 'the rules of the game' and ways of negotiating contacts with criminal justice agencies, remain crucially important. Why, when so many years have been spent developing the technique, should they abandon a game where the rules have only just been grasped?

Nevertheless important changes do occur in this intermediate stage from adolescence to adulthood, as the accounts of Del, Jimmy, and Barry and those of the older group of contemporary youths will reveal. These changes involve a shift from the highly visible public sphere of crime, which is the preserve of youths, to the private and institutionalised sphere during adulthood. Other research has also pointed to changes in the type of criminal acts and the attitudes offenders have towards them in later stages of the life cycle. Shover's (1985) research for example on 'ageing property thieves' in the United States suggests that patterns of offending change in adulthood becoming less confrontational and less visible. He wrote:

> Aging ordinary property offenders describe, albeit in a variety of terms, experientially subtle but fundamental changes they can see in themselves. They said that they had become 'more settled', 'more mature', 'softer' and 'more responsible.
>
> (Shover 1985: 79)

Shover (1985) argues that these changes occur in middle age as offenders 'take stock of their lives and ... [realise] that crime was an unproductive enterprise'. The result of this 'stock take' is that offenders develop what Shover calls a 'modified calculus' where they engage in less serious crime, as Figure 5 illustrates.

Figure 5 Links among ageing, changing perspectives, the changing criminal calculus, and criminal behaviour

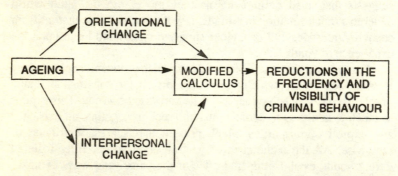

Luckenbill and Best (1981: 204) also suggest that offenders resort to less risky forms of crime as a result of evaluating their behaviour. A drug addict, for example, may shift from burglary to dealing in drugs in order to finance his habit (cf Smith and Stephans 1976) because

'exchange' 'reduce[s] uncertainty, regularize[s] rewards [and] . . . often produces regular profits.' In the case of Del and his contemporaries the shift from public to private occurred due to a combination of new opportunities which emerged at adulthood and a reflection on their juvenile pasts, as the following discussion indicates.

The world of work: new opportunities

Although the transition from school to work is not a dramatic one in working-class culture because of the boring and repetitive nature of much manual work (cf Downes 1966, Willis 1977), the occupational setting provides a variety of new opportunities to satisfy the pursuit of 'easy money'. Jimmy's 'career' is the best illustration of the way in which the world of work can be exploited to the full. He began his working life repairing fishing reels, and his hidden economy activities began as soon as he arrived.

> I got four pounds ten bob a week repairing fishing reels, although I made just as much by nicking the bits and taking them home and making fishing reels [there], as I did by me wages.

Jimmy's life from this point on was characterised by his hidden economic activity in the various jobs he occupied. During the years of his apprenticeship training to be an engineer, he worked for a bread firm and an electronics firm (he was sacked from the latter for stealing from work). He got involved in fights and football violence, as well as stealing radios, cassettes and other articles from cars, and driving without tax, insurance etc. Between 16 and 20, the age that he married, he describes his life thus:

Jimmy: I got taken up the magistrates court a couple of times, well several times. . . . Whatever you could get away with at the time you done. It was as simple as that.

JF: So how did you feel on these successive occasions when you went in front of the magistrate?

Jimmy: Determined that I wasn't gonna get caught the next time. They'd done me once, they'd outwitted me once, I never got caught for the same thing twice, it was always somethink else but in the same line.

Note that Jimmy says nothing here that indicates he had any intention of giving up his activities, as others who have focused on juvenile delinquency suggest. When I asked him if he had made any commitments not to do it again, he told me:

> You make so many commitments sayin' 'I'm not gonna do that now, I'm finished with that' and umm 'Cor that doesn't half look nice dunnit, I think I'll have that.'

The most essential ingredient in understanding why these practices continued to thrive was that in an environment where the fruits of criminal activities were accepted they were seen as quite legitimate avenues to goods which people might not otherwise afford (Roselius and Benton 1973). Yet simply because 'easy money' was obtained with relative ease, it was often conspicuously consumed, and as a result people were always in pursuit of it.

Unemployment has often been cited as a crucial element in the commission of crime and urban unrest (cf Brake 1985, Haslam undated, Farrington *et al*. 1986). For those I have described here unemployment was not a major problem (nor was it for the contemporary youths because of extended family networks). However, the jobs that Del and his friends (and those which most unqualified school leavers obtain) are very poorly paid so that while the job market was reasonably buoyant in the 1960s (and Barry was the only one who was unemployed for any significant period (when he was AWOL) it was during paid employment that Del, Jimmy, and Barry supplemented their income in various ways by thieving. Del, for example, stole money for his leisure pursuits. He told me:

Del:	I was goin' on the old buildin' sites when I ain't got no money and I want to sit indoors with a bottle of beer or wanna go down the pub or go to football, whatever. The easiest way I felt I could do it then was goin' out and stealin' it. You couldn't work for it.
JF	Because there was no work?
Del:	I've always had work, but the money was never very good, the money was never any good.

A NACRO questionnaire (cf Haslam undated) administered to ten West Indian youths reported that those who had 'been involved in quite a bit of crime' felt that only a job with sufficient rewards would stop their offending. As they held high expectations (in instrumental terms) and little opportunity of achieving them, crime remained a legitimate avenue. The author concluded:

It is my opinion that criminal activities are discussed at length especially among the older groups (16-20 onwards). It came out in discussion that nothing will deter young blacks from committing crimes other than jobs and consequently a good standard of living. Imprisonment and other sentences are not a deterrent at all as they are willing to do 'their bird'. (Haslam undated: 4–5)

A number of studies have indicated that delinquency is related to employment history, as offenders are often found in low-status occupations and seem to change their jobs more frequently (Bottoms and McClintock 1973, West 1982, Ferguson 1952) Both the adult and older teenagers in this research experienced rapid employment turnover and poorly paid, low-status work (see Chap 5).

The pursuit of easy money

Hobbs (1988) has argued that East End working-class culture is characterised by an entrepreneurial spirit which has existed for centuries, where any means of making money, legitimate or otherwise, will be exploited. These activities are dictated by market forces where involvement in entrepreneurial activity provides a feeling of control and excitement for participants. Hobbs captures the age-old dilemma in talking about crime and rationality (since it doesn't actually pay in the long run) by emphasising that although people think that they will make money from 'normal crime', such ventures often end up taking high risks for little financial reward (personal conversation).

Matza and others assume that, at the point of adulthood, rationality enters the minds of those who continue to pursue criminal activities. As Del argues below, the pursuit of easy money overrides any rational considerations of the likelihood of getting caught or any question of moral wrongness in the act .

If it's easy pickings, [like] the building sites, they don't sit down and think hang on a minute if we go and nick these tools and sell 'em for twenty quid, now for twenty quid what are the consequences, we could get two years, is it worth having two years for that twenty quid? They don't think on those terms, they would think, is it easy, yeah it's easy, the risk isn't all that great of us gettin' nicked, yeah we'll try it. Then if they get nicked they can think what the consequences were. 'Silly of us doin' that for 20 quid!'

The emphasis was therefore placed on the ease with which opportunistic crimes could be committed and on those whose property was stolen, as they had not made stealing more difficult. Del, for example, argued

> The building sites, it was so easy. . . . You'd waste [hundreds] of pounds to get yer sort of five or ten quids worth of scrap. It's laughable. But it's the sort of thing you can do. Once you've got it anybody'll accept it in the scrap game. Copper, brass, lead. It was easy, it wasn't criminal. It was stupidity on the part of the building sites. I think they've got more sense now they've got the dogs. I mean that's what eventually deterred me from going back.

The search for excitement, which was expressed in youth in the activities on the street from breaking bottles to thieving, begins during these years to become more institutionalised and focused on particular areas which provide accessible outlets for easy money, where stolen goods can be readily sold with little risk. Such activities remain, as they were in youth, episodic.

Parameters of activity

Barry had been involved in and caught for the 'heaviest villainy' and when he was released from Detention Centre drifted into a café clique (regarded as the 'in place for villains' at the time) and continued his activities. However, he realised after a short time that the behaviour of the café clique was 'too heavy' and decided to join Del's crowd who were involved only in 'medium things'. This formed part of an evaluation process which occurred at the intermediary stage and was influenced by the experience of getting caught and the emergence of networks which could satisfy the pursuit of easy money with less risk. I will describe this in more detail in Chapter 5, but would like to concentrate here on Barry's interpretation of his behaviour. Soon after leaving Detention Centre, Barry joined the army, which, he believed, 'put a stop to a lot of it',

> cos you're governed in there – you've gotta do every hour by every hour. It's ruled for yer. They tell yer to walk, you walk, they tell yer to march, you march. Everything's set out for yer, you got a programme. At the end of it you're gonna get paid, you're gonna get yer time off. You get around, I went three-quarters of the way round the world, I'd never do that if I wasn't in the army.

Miller (1958) in his analysis of lower-class culture highlighted an important irony which is expressed in Barry's comments above, where there is a conflict between the wish for autonomy and the wish to be ruled. Miller wrote:

> On the overt level there is a strong and frequently expressed resentment of the idea of external controls, restrictions on behaviour and unjust and coercive authority ... [but] being controlled is [also equated] with being cared for. ... Many lower class people appear to seek out highly restrictive social environments wherein stringent external controls are maintained over their behaviour. ... Having been released, or having escaped from these milieux, however, he will often act in such a way as to insure recommitment, or choose recommitment voluntarily after a temporary period of 'freedom'.
>
> (Miller 1958: 12–13)

For Barry this was very much the case. During his years in the army he spent six months in an army prison and a substantial period of time AWOL (absent without leave).

Del argued that Barry had 'a lot more bottle' (courage) than himself and believed his own activities from youth to his late 20s ' never got any worse'. He said:

> All right stealing a bottle of lemonade is one thing, breakin' and enterin' is another, but goin' further than that I don't s'pose I really had the bottle to start breakin' into warehouses or things like that. I don't think it progressed, just sort of come along at a steady pace I s'pose, [I] just sort of dwelled there.

Jimmy set the parameters of activity at anything that could earn him money and argued that between 16 and 20 his activities were getting 'steadily worse'. 'If I hadn't got married then I don't know what would have happened' he said.

Although there is no conclusive evidence that marriage has a significant influence on the reduction of deviant activity, it is often described as a positive step towards adulthood and responsibility and leads to a reduction in peer group activity (cf Parker 1976). The effects of marriage in my opinion are at best short term, but may be influential in the initial period after marriage. Wives often had little information or knowledge of their husbands' activities (until they were apprehended: see Chapter 4) and while they liked to believe they possessed the power to reform their husbands, they knew in reality that they had little influence or deterrent value. Although Jimmy maintained that marriage inhibited his behaviour he was still 'doin' business':

> Anythink that was goin', if I wanted it,. . . don't matter what, if we needed it, thanks very much, give 'em the money for it or if I had somethink and somebody wanted it, you know the same.

Barry emphasised the responsibilities of marriage and children but, while it is true that his activities declined in seriousness, his life was far from trouble free. Yet he argued that marriage

> Gives yer a bit of responsibility don't it. I mean Sal was pregnant and you tone yerself down. I still got meself in a little bit of trouble in the army, that's only through drinkin' and messing around in general, just silly things nothink serious. . . . I wasn't hangin' around with 'em cos I had to go out and earn a livin' to pay for me rent and the bills and things like that. I could have done it thieving but there's no way I'll go back in, when I've got him on the way and she's sittin' there. It wouldn't be very nice for her. If I was single then, it might have been different, I might have been doin' five years now.

Barry's comments are rather ironic, since he was released from army detention on a special licence to marry Sal! Del, on the other hand, argued that, although marriage mellowed him, it did not deter him.

> I think it mellowed me, I don't think it deterred me cos when we was first married we didn't have a lot. Well we didn't have piss all. When I talk about going on the building sites . . . on the money I got from that we'd enjoy ourselves. When you've got no money and it's easy stealings like that, you know, if I were in the same situation now I'd go and steal the same way.

Contacts with official agencies.

I argued earlier that initial contacts with law-enforcement agencies had a fearful component as offenders are unsure of the system and what might happen to them. In the intermediary stage attitudes towards the police and other criminal justice agencies hardened because initial prejudice was confirmed. However, despite the antagonism in encounters with the police, there was in contrast to youth a predictability about encounters and expectations of behaviour because Del and his friends had learned the rules of the game and how to play them.

An incident which involved Barry and Del illustrates this well. Barry had been involved in a car accident in a vehicle he had stolen from a garage forecourt. When he was taken to hospital he gave Del's name and address and the police duly arrived at Del's flat to inform Chris that he was in the hospital. Although Del was actually sitting in the living room, she gave no indication of this to the police officer. Del described the incident:

> I'm sittin' in the other room, but it must be somebody who knows me so I've gotta go and find out. We get there and it's Barry, arms and legs all over the place. I don't know whether he wasn't expecting me or didn't know he had given me name or what, but as soon as I walked up he's started callin' me Del and I'm callin' him Barry, and in that situation you've always got a police officer sitting by the bed, so the copper's going 'Who?' and then you don't say nothink to each other do yer.

As in youth, episodes where individuals had 'got one over on the Old Bill' were repeated with fervour. Barry and Del again provided the best example.

> We decided to go on the building site and we nicked all this copper [and] . . . we drove it back to where [Del] used to live. It was all in the car, all bent up like and covered by sack to take to the scrap yard the next morning. We were sittin' in the car havin' a cigarette and a policeman walked past, and he see all this sack in the back. He said, 'What have yer got in the back? So me and Del, we were all the same, you know, you got caught so you tell 'em. So we said 'Ah brand new copper tube, we nicked it off the building site and bent it up and stuffed it under the sack.' The copper laughed and walked away, he didn't believe us and there was somethink like 300 quids worth underneath . . . we thought it was hilarious.
>
> (Barry)

Not all encounters ended with such results, and it was on the occasions where formal contact led to arrest that attitudes hardened. One particular case involving Barry and Del had consequences for both parties. It clearly illustrates some of the underlying feelings of perceived misjustice that is experienced by those who receive attention from the police. Del told me:

> We decided we was gonna nick this lead off the church. . . . I sent Barry off to get the car but I'm not gonna leave this lead, so I've shouldered it over a fence to try and hide cos I've now heard the police are coming, but I'm still not gonna leave this lead – that's mine. The police did come, they threw me in their van and hauled me down the station. I must have been in the place for four or five hours. I think it's just a waste you know, cos once they've got yer and they know you. You've got the lead so you've done something wrong, you've nicked it, I mean you didn't grow it did yer! You didn't just go 'Cooh blimey there's a load of lead just fell on me.' But the time wasting, whereas somethink like that you're red handed, you couldn't plead not guilty if yer wanted to. You just couldn't, well I couldn't. But being locked up for that five hours with nothink done really starts making yer boil, you know why, what's it all about. Anyhow the normal rigmarole – empty yer pockets and all the rest of it and I've got Barry's army ID card on me (he was AWOL at the time). . . . He's done the big brother bit I s'ppose to come down and get me and as soon as he's walked in they've sort of gone, 'Who are you' and he's gone 'Peter . . .' and they've shown him the ID card and said 'Well who's this?' So he said 'That's me broffer', first mistake, it's got Barry . . . wrote on the ID card and he's Peter . . ., and 'Whose in there then?' 'Del. . . .' They said 'Yeah that's the name he gave us in all but who's this?' So with that he's put his hands up and they've let me out, locked him up and I'm away. I mean I've still been charged but I'm on the way out.[2]

Having some appreciation of Del's attitude to an 'honest cop' (which is not to say that if they can find a loophole they won't use it) it is perhaps easy to understand why when people are set up by the police they are angry and grow to resent the law even more, because they are powerless to do anything about it. Del continued:

> The very next day I'm in court. I think I got a £20 or £30 fine for the lead thing, back on the street no problem. The very next day I was walkin' past the place I got nicked with the lead. Just remember I've been nicked, in the court, walking past the same place next day. The police come along and say 'What do yer want

to be nicked for, drugs or cars?' I said 'Yer kiddin' ain't yer ?' They said 'Well start laughing, we're goin' down the station.' Now I'm lunatic, there's no way I'm gonna have that. Eventually they've got me down the station and I'm screamin' and hollerin' and kickin' and biting and fightin'. . . . In the end he come up [the policeman] and said, 'You might as well tell him, they're gonna nick yer anyway.' A couple of hours go by and they've come in and gone 'Right we'll do yer for cars.' I said 'I've got three cars of me own why would I want to steal a car?' 'We see yer touch the door handle of one.' They've charged me and they've done the bit and then said 'Right, off yer go.' For the first time in me life I've been nicked for somethink I didn't do and there's a bit of an edge comin', one way or other I'm gonna get even.[3]

Del hired a solicitor but lost the case at court:

We've got in the court and the copper's got up in the stand. I've gone off me rocker that he can stand in there and lie. I wouldn't do that, I wouldn't get in the box and lie, it's just a thing about it, you know, you're caught and that's it. It really got me that he could get up there and lie his way through it and that's a copper for yer . . . I've gone a bit barmy. Needless to say I was fined £50 and found guilty and I kicked the chairs all over the place. I was lucky I didn't get nicked for somethink I did do, like contempt of court or whatever. It's just that these sort of attitudes should be noted, people don't go like that if they've done somethink wrong and they've been found guilty they'll just walk off. They might say 'I'll get even with yer' or whatever else. They don't sort of smash the place up and say coppers are lyin' and everythink else. If somebody gives yer a kick up the nuts before the law, respect for the law for me then just went sssh – no more, no more will you get any sense out of me. Since then even now my attitude is very much the same, there's no way I'd lie, bend, anythink, there's no way they'll get anything out of me. That's the only time I've been up in front when I haven't done anything. It really is, when you go to court and you've done somethink wrong, all right you're frightened, you know you've got somethink comin', but you don't know what it is. But when you go and you've done nothink ohh that's somethink else.

Del was on first-name terms with most of the local police officers at this time and they regularly raided his home (see Chapter 5). But his relationship with them changed over the years through his businesses. He became the focus for more specialist branches where behaviour was sometimes brutal but there were more openings for negotiation.

Perceived changes: twenty years on

The previous discussion illustrates that distinctions between juvenile and adult crime may not be as dramatic and clear cut as they are often portrayed. It reveals a large grey area between the professional criminal world and the law-abiding one, where duckin' and divin' continues in an episodic fashion for men even in their late 30s: there is no commitment to give up crime since 'there is nothing wrong with it as long as you don't get caught'. The final part of this chapter will bring the attitudes, behaviour, and experiences of Jimmy, Barry, and Del into the present-day context, describing the changes they perceive in themselves.

A new sense of worth

One of the most important transitions in the adult years is a belief that behaviour is more thoughtful and rational, and that the consequences of getting caught have resulted in a re-evaluation of behaviour and an adoption of strategies to avoid getting caught again. As Barry argued:

> I think DC was the best thing they ever done for me and I think it could well be for a lot of other people [but] DC didn't stop yer doin' it, you just didn't get captured. I never got caught for a lot of things after I came out of DC, you learn too much off of other people in there. When you come out you think about what you're gonna do, do it a little bit shrewder [and] you make sure you're a little bit more careful.

Although all the adults believed their present behaviour differed from their youth, attitudes and behaviour often differed. They argued, for example, that the pursuit of easy money, breaking and entering, fighting, and thieving were a thing of the past, yet in many cases, their behaviour remained episodic but was framed in a language which minimised their actions and somehow excused the occasions when they had misbehaved. Jimmy serves as an excellent example:

[Fighting] don't do that now. Mind you, don't get me wrong, we used to be in some scrapes, not so long ago I was in another scrape. But that's neither here nor there really. Silly things like spur of the moment things.

This 'scrape' which Jimmy explains as being 'neither here nor there' was a serious assault on two black men. He was charged and appeared in court for this incident.

This new sense of worth which Del, Jimmy, and Barry expressed was related to a belief that they had learnt the lesson that crime in most circumstances does not pay so they would engage in it only if it offered the potential for large sums of money. As Del pointed out, 'If I get locked up for one week, it's got to be worth at least five hundred pounds a week for me', whilst Barry said 'If I'm gonna do five years I'm gonna do it for a lot more than I was offered. If I'm gonna spend a year in nick I want twenty grand a year when I'm in there and I want it outside.' Shover (1985) notes similar trends among his sample of ageing criminals. He argued that 'as offenders age, their expectations of the potential outcome of criminal acts changes,' and while they still *think* about crime, 'they develop a more complex set of reasons for avoiding it.' Yet just like Del, Jimmy, and Barry, the lure was always there, as one of his respondents told him:

Now I'm not going to tell you that if you put $100,000 on that table and I saw an opportunity, that I felt I could get away with it, that I wouldn't try to move it. But there's no way ... I would endanger my freedom for a measly four, five, ten thousand dollars.

(Shover 1985: 115)

However, the theory of this new sense of worth and the practice were often very different. As Parker's conversations with a white collar fraudster reveal,

Oh no, it deters in no way whatsoever. All that does happen is that you make up your mind either that you'll take damn good care next time you won't be caught; or if you are, it's going to be for something worth while. In other words, if you're going to get ten years for fifty pounds, you might as well make it five hundred or five thousand pounds. Though, of course, no one really functions along these lines at all, outside: the last thing in any criminal's mind at the time he's committing an offence is that he's going to get anything for it. He's quite certain he's not going to get anything for it, because he's not going to get caught.

(Parker 1967: 108)

Episodic contacts with official agencies continued for Del, Jimmy, and Barry therefore throughout their 20s and into their 30s. Their attitudes, however, remained the same, as their accounts illustrate below.

Jimmy

> Over the last few years I have been lucky, things I've done, things I've got away with, luckier now, than what I was when I was younger. They say being wise comes with age. . . . I just got I wouldn't say cleverer, cos I still got caught a couple of times, . . . but I'm wiser now, I do things that hopefully wouldn't get me caught. . . . I think a lot more about it before I actually do it. I didn't used to: I just used to jump in head first. . . . Time has mellowed me. I look for the reason as well as why it should happen now I didn't before, it happened and that's it. Now I look: could we have avoided it, if we can avoid it and whoops, shouldn't we have avoided it?

Jimmy was the least successful of the three men and was most certainly a loser. Since his mid-20s he had had two court appearances, one for theft from work, the other for assault, but was fortunate not to have had more, since he was arrested several times in this period. He still stole lead from roofs and parts from cars in addition to his work-related exploits, for which he had been caught on many occasions (he was sacked twice in the space of two months for pilfering just after the research finished).

Although Jimmy maintained that he had been luckier as the years had progressed and had, despite his failures, received less attention from official agencies, this was not, in reality, due to his greater care or thought, but because of the more private sphere within which he operated as an adult. The two incidents where he was prosecuted both involved outside agencies because of the nature of the crimes: the first was a blatant assault in a public place; in the second the police had actually been called in to deal with a theft from an electrical company where Jimmy worked .

Whilst he would have liked things to be different, they were in fact still very much the same. This is particularly important when we consider statements such as the one below, statements which at first glance appear to show a distinct change.

I have less inclination now to do anythink like that [criminal] solely because if I lose that I lose me job and I wouldn't want to lose anythink else.

Jimmy was referring to Carol and their children when he said he 'wouldn't like to lose anythink else'. Yet, as is so often the case, the distance between words and actions was great: within weeks of this statement Jimmy had lost his job and his treatment of Carol towards the end of the research and after became much worse.[4]

Jimmy suffered from severe status frustration, aware that others around him had fared much better. He was very impressed with the 'playboy world' of fast cars, beautiful women, and money, but these were far removed from his own and Carol's existence in their little pre-war council flat. Although there had been times in his life when he had earned quite considerable amounts of money (see Chapter 2) this had been frittered away with very little to show for it.

Jimmy's frustration and jealousy often prompted vindictive acts, for which he always found justification. On one occasion he arranged for two friends to steal, dismantle, and scrap Carol's first husband's car, because he was angry that her previous husband had kept it when they were separated. This is the car that Jimmy describes as mysteriously going 'missing' in the extract below. At about the same time he also discovered that his first wife had been having an affair with someone who worked in the same firm as him (he'd had several affairs himself by this time). Jimmy's description aptly illustrates how he deflected the blame on to these totally extraneous factors, in order to detract from his own direct involvement in the enterprise.

I was workin' at [company] . . . anythink that was goin' I bought cos it was [good] stuff and you could sell it. A tape recorder deck, a new one, beautiful thing it was. Somebody bought it up and said, 'Do yer want it Jim?' cos they must have been able to nick 'em right left and centre at this place. Now during this time her old man's car's gone missing, now whether he had it in for us I don't know, or whether somebody actually see me bringing this home, [but] on Saturday morning the coppers come round and raided the house, took her away [see Chapter 4]. I didn't go back . . . after that because the Friday I found out about [first wife's lover] and on the Saturday me place got done. . . . I got fined £50 and that was that. . . . Lucky really, cos what I had me eye on, that somebody was gonna get for me, was one of those 7 inch reel to reel upright tape decks, they was about a thousand pounds and to say I was in love with it would be an understatement, I would have given my right arm for it. If I'd had one of them I've no doubt they would have put me away.

Barry

I've grown up. 34 I'm now, I ain't 16 no more. I ain't got to tear around, fly around, I've got a good job, I've got two cars, I've got a house and I enjoy what I'm doin'. I still go out and have a drink with me mates and stuff like that. If some't came up for the right price then yeah, why not?

Sal was instrumental to Barry's relative success in his adult years. She had encouraged him to lead a more stable life style, and tried to moderate his views and activities. She, for example, suggested he stopped scaffolding and became a supervisor, which, although less lucrative in good weather, provided a steady income. Yet despite certain changes, Barry's attitudes remained very similar. This was illustrated during the research when Barry appeared in court for assualting a black man who worked on a scaffolding team with him. Barry's description of the incident reveals all the rationalizations of earlier years:

Barry: ABH. Yeah that was just trouble in work, a personal argument, the geezer didn't like a bit of authority . . . so he took a swing at me and I hit him back and he fell forward and cut his face and the police went absolutely against me.

JF: Why did they go against you?

Barry: I dunno. They never really asked me what happened. They just told me I was gonna be nicked, very abrupt cos that's the sort of thing they are now, very abrupt, very rubbish policemen now. They don't seem to have the authority and they think the only way they can get it back is to treat yer like pigs. I mean it was a bit embarrassing, I got stripped in the cell and all me bits taken away from me . . . get a charge sheet, yer photos, yer prints and then they come back and tell yer

what they've got on record, well that don't bother me
anyway. But the guy that's actually done it [the man
Barry hit] he's been done for ABH twice and
malicious wounding and stuff like that.

JF: So why did they choose to prosecute you?

Barry: I haven't got a clue. I won't know until I go to court,
until the solicitor sorts it out. . . . I'm actually pushing
to go to Crown Court cos I want to absolutely
prosecute the police for wrongful arrest.

Barry's injustice centred around his perception that the police had
prosecuted the wrong man and were 'rubbish' because of that. Rather
amusingly, after the court case (which Barry won) he changed his mind
about the police and said that they had been quite helpful. Although on
face value it would seem that attitudes towards criminal justice agencies
on the one hand were always accusatory and cynical, as other writers
have been at pains to point out, individual officers and certain cases (see
Chapter 5) could be exceptions to this general rule. However, in terms
of this present discussion, what is important is that Barry did not at any
point accept his own culpability in the procedings. The police had
prosecuted him because he had assaulted the man! These attitudes differ
little from those outlined by Matza for juveniles.

The cases of Jimmy and Barry illustrate the continued marginality in
adult years. From time to time in the future they will continue to have
brushes with authority. Del's adult development, however, took a more
ambitious path.

Del

My ways changed but not necessarily me attitude, I still wouldn't
let anybody take liberties with me.

Del was undoubtedly the most successful of the three men. From his
early days of burglary, thieving, and street fighting, the building sites
and scrap yards, he had become a successful businessman with
substantial connections. Each night he drove past the scrap yard on his
way home from the pub and if he caught anyone in the yard, did exactly
what had been done to him – 'threatened 'em'. As the discussion in
Chapter 3 indicated, Del did not believe that his present activities
(receiving stolen goods) constituted crime, but there were others,
particularly the police, who believed they did. During the fieldwork

period he was arrested on several occasions, but only one case resulted in prosecution.

Summary

This chapter has focused on the formation of juvenile and adult attitudes through the histories of Del, Jimmy, and Barry. Several conclusions can be drawn from this discussion about the nature of attitudes and their relationship to behaviour. The first is that attitudes towards crime and law enforcement relate to actual experience. Whilst the parent generation create an atmosphere where such experiences receive confirmation, they do not directly determine them (cf Chapters 5 and 6). Attitudes towards the police were on the whole accusatory and antagonistic, although there was also a nostalgic belief in the old-type copper. Fear of the police was more immediate than that of the juvenile courts and influenced attitudes about the way in which offenders should be dealt with. The law was supposed to be hard and to act as a deterrent; instead it was weak and ineffectual. None of the measures, violent or otherwise, actually deterred behaviour, because the pursuit of easy money overcame any rational assessment of whether crime was worthwhile or not. The juvenile years were characterised by learning the rudimentary rules, where getting caught teaches offenders how not to get caught again. The onset of adulthood marked a shift from the public to the private sphere of crime and allowed the greater exploitation of local opportunity structures with less likelihood of detection.

Notes

1   Laurie Taylor (1985: 129) describes an incident where John McVicar gave a lecture to some probation officers. 'At the end of the talk one of them stood up and congratulated him on his book. This, he said, he had found very moving. It had greatly helped him understand why John became involved in crime, and the struggle to overcome his criminal predilections. However, he had detected in the film a much cruder approach. In the film he merely seemed to be enjoying himself when he was out robbing banks and on the run. How could he explain the difference? Was the film untrue? "Well" John had replied, not I suspect without a certain enjoyment. "That's exactly as it should have been. Because you see, the book with all its accounts of childhood and causes was written originally as my defence statement, when I'd been picked up after the escape. It was really written for people like probation officers. So I'm glad you liked it. The film, on the other hand, was a bit more about how it really was."

2 Del's notion of the lead being 'his' is aptly described by Tannenbaum (1938: 174) who quoted Jack Black as saying: 'Respect for property in the underworld is as deep as it is in the upper world. The fact that it's upperworld property which is involved makes no difference, for when property is transferred from the upperworld to the underworld it becomes sacred again.'

3 Such practices are documented by many criminals (see Parker and Allerton 1962) and during my own observations with the police, some officers readily admitted such practices. One officer at Stanton told me that the area car driver held up a packet of cannabis and some car keys and told him 'We'll get you a body tonight'.

4 Del described an incident which occurred on a darts holiday which indicates a great deal about Jimmy and his behaviour. He told me:

> I lost all respect for the man when we was on holiday. I went round to the chalet and he literally slagged Carol off and told her that he was gonna smash her in the face in my company. Now I wouldn't care if he does or don't, I don't care . . .behind the door he can smash her to bits but you don't ever mention it in front of me. That is when I totally went, . . . once I heard that I can't have any other opinion except he's a pig. . . things'll never change with him.

Chapter four

Women

The preceding chapters have addressed both the theoretical issues concerned with crime and the community and the ethnographic material relating to the attitudes and patterns of offending among the adult generation. This discussion has focused entirely on men. Although women have often received scant attention from observers of working-class culture they in fact play a crucial role in the transmission of values from one generation to the next. This chapter therefore focuses on the women in the Grafton Arms, whose biographies highlight important gender differences in both adolescent and adult experience.

Working-class culture and the extended family

Considerable changes in family patterns have occurred in post-war years (cf Young and Willmott 1957, Klein 1965, Bott 1957, Goldthorpe *et al.* 1969, Dennis *et al.* 1956) with trends away from 'traditional' working-class life styles (characterised by extended family patterns, little mobility, and highly segregated role relationships) to more aspiring and home-centred life styles with greater sharing of roles and less reliance on the family. Yet the lives of Del and his contemporaries, and those of the younger generation, were still dominated by the values and traditions of established working-class communities. Although there were differences between grandparents and parents in attitudes towards children, punishment, and family size, for example, the adult generation's way of life was still dominated by the wish to preserve and reproduce cultural traditions. Most of the adults lived within a few streets of their parents and close relatives, and visited them regularly. The matriarchal structure (cf Kerr 1958, Young and Willmott 1957, Bott

1957, Klein 1965) remained as important as it was in the South London which Firth and Djamour described in the 1950s:

> this woman is a key figure in South Borough kinship. In terms of emotional relationship, communication and services ... the tie between a mother and her children is normally very strong, and tends to remain so throughout her life. Mother and married daughter are commonly in frequent, often daily, contact, and a married son also tends to visit his mother at least weekly, if possible.
>
> (Firth and Djamour 1956: 41)

The existence of close kinship networks and their consequent impact on reproducing traditional values resulted in the family being the primary focus of attention for the Grafton women. It formed the major support network and served many of the functions fulfilled by friends in middle-class households (cf Young and Willmott 1957). Joanne, for example, explained that her family were 'really close' and said of the women in the darts team:

> They're not what I call a friend. [A friend] you see regularly, like everyday, or go shopping with 'em, and you know their families and you tell 'em things. They're not friends like that. If I was to speak about 'em, I'd probably say 'Me friend came yesterday and she done an interview', but they wouldn't be what I'd call true friends cos I hardly know 'em. I see 'em once a week and that's it.

Bott (1957) argued that for women in this kind of culture, 'friends were either neighbours or relatives.'

Although the matriarchal structure had an important impact on friendship networks in its own right, women often lost contact with their female peers when they left school (Griffin 1984), which served to strengthen and reinforce reliance on the extended family structure.

Although the relationship between mother and daughter is probably the strongest bond, the family was also influential in the lives of fathers and sons, particularly for securing employment (cf Young and Willmott 1957, Wallman 1982). As Young and Willmott (1962: 102) argued: 'wherever father works with son and brother with brother, the men have a link the counterpart of the women's. Family and workplace are intertwined.' Children often worked in the same occupations as their parents, so jobs in the docks, the print, and markets were all characterised by 'family succession'. The relationship between family, and employment was most marked in Jimmy's family as he indicates below:

> I could have started work on the papers same as me dad, brother John worked [for] the Jones' [name of firm] me sister Betty worked on the Jones', brother-in-law worked on the paper, me sister Vicky on Jones'. Sandra worked at Jones', everyone except me fuckin' mother, who worked at the pickle factory round the corner!

Relationships between men and women

Extended family patterns and a firm attachment to tradition had an important influence on the nature of relationships between men and women in the Grafton, which remained extremely traditional. The men spent most of their evenings in the pub and even when husbands and wives went to the Grafton or any other social gathering together (normally organised by the women) they rarely mixed. At parties men would congregate near the drink and engage in 'men's talk' (football, 'doin' business', etc) while the women would dance, play hostess, or sit quietly in a corner. There was no outward display of affection, and once the first flourish of romance had disappeared, spouses were simply tolerated. As Jimmy's observations before the demise of his own relationship with Carol confirm:

> I kiss and cuddle her in the pub. . . never see Del do it to Chris. They know a lot more about each other than me and Carol do, because they've been together so long. So they understand each other. I won't say love's gone out of the winda, but they understand each other a lot more than what we do . . . see the newness hasn't worn off for me and her yet.

Gans (1962) argued that in such relationships 'husbands and wives come together for procreation, and sexual gratification, but less so for the mutual satisfaction of emotional needs or problem solving.'

It was assumed that the sexes had little in common and nothing to talk about, as they had different needs and interests (cf Dennis *et al.* 1956). Joanne, for example, argued that while she didn't like her husband going out 'a lot of times, if he's home we don't talk so he might as well be out.' Bott noted a similar tendency and concluded:

> Mr and Mrs Newbolt took it for granted that men had male

interests and women have female interests and that there were few leisure activities they could naturally share.

(Bott, 1957: 73)

In some cases these separate interests were also pursued on holiday and at the annual darts week which the clique attended at a seaside resort, the men and women (with the children of course!) separated for the majority of the time. Chris explained that 'they would be bored otherwise' and argued that if she and Del went away on holiday alone they would have 'nothing to talk about.' Children were often the only reason why couples stayed together.

Sal was the only woman who differed in her attitude and expectations of relationships. She did not accept that they had to be segregated and wanted to do things jointly with Barry. Her attitudes were largely derived from the experience of her own parents. She told me:

> I've always liked to do what my mum and dad have done. I mean even now, all right I go out Tuesdays, my mum and dad have never been out separately. ... my mum used to think it was terrible cos [Barry] used to go out when I had the kids quite young. ... [Barry] says 'Go on go' and I say 'No, I don't wanna.' I mean if [Barry] could take me and go with me it would be all right. [Barry] says 'Come on, go out' but I don't wanna not without him or the kids.

Barry said:

> The things I do you can't do with two. There's no way she likes standin' in the pub with the smoke where I talk about motors and racing and golf. She sits in the corner and the only time she enjoys it is when we go playin' darts. I used to go motor racing and I used to have to drag her, the only reason she went was because the kids went.

Expectations about the behaviour of spouses tended to be reproduced from generation to generation. Carol's toleration of Jimmy's behaviour, for example, was rooted in her observation and understanding of her parents' relationship.

> Me dad don't come home sometimes til closing. At least Jimmy will come home and have his dinner [after] work; me dad don't, he'll go straight to the pub.[1]

The generational replication of highly divided role models was, I believe, based on generational emulation. Unlike attitudes towards crime and offending, which were developed as a result of independent experience, the reproduction of gender roles occurred because of the differing socialisation and expectations to which both males and females were subjected from an early age. Some of these issues will be discussed later in the chapter.

The girls' night out

Unlike their male counterparts the women had always led very restricted lives with little freedom or room for self-expression. They were all prematurely aged and often looked tired and worn down by family commitments and domestic responsibilities. Mary McIntosh's (1978) comment seems most apt in this regard: 'pub recreation is there for the needs of the tired and working man, no one asks how the tired and working woman manages.' For many, their weekly darts night was the only evening they went out, but for this brief period, the women claimed public bar territory and jealously guarded it from both men and outsiders. They took great delight in humiliating and teasing any unfortunate men who ventured across their territory. The emphasis, like that of their male counterparts, was on escapism, where 'being one of the girls' and having fun were greatly facilitated by drink. They rarely talked about the mundane problems of day-to-day life.

Although some of the women enjoyed playing darts, the game itself was of secondary importance. Primarily, playing darts provided the women with a legitimate reason for a night out and was an activity with which their husbands and boyfriends could identify. This was illustrated during a big league competition, where play continued into the early hours of the morning. Many of the women were too drunk to stand up, let alone aim their darts! Hen nights, arranged twice yearly, also provided a release from the day-to-day drudgery, where cheap thrills were provided by male strippers and large amounts of alcohol were consumed. However, all 'nights out' had to be legitimised, so that there should be no suspicion that any woman was having an affair. Joanne, for example, was not seen for several weeks after the darts match mentioned above, as Billy would not believe she was playing darts until the early hours of the morning.

Men and women: action versus routine

Highly segregated role relationships not only reflected the differing interests of men and women but also highlighted differences in their attitudes and values as well. Gans's distinctions between 'routine-seekers' and 'action-seekers' summed up the gender differences here.

> The routine-seekers are people whose aim is the establishment of a stable way of living, in which the economic and emotional security of the individual and his family are most important. Their way of life is characterised by highly regular and recurring scheduling of behaviour and organized routine. . . . For the action-seeker life is episodic. The rhythm of life is dominated by the adventurous episode . . . of immediate gratification.
>
> (Gans 1962: 28–9)

Gans argued that action-seeking was an entirely male pursuit, but routine-seeking was not exclusively female. However, in terms of the adults in this research action- and routine-seeking could be divided by gender alone. It was an ongoing battle for the women to maintain familial links and emotional and physical well-being, in the face of their husbands' often irresponsible action-seeking. Although they tried to encourage routine-seeking behaviour in their men, it met with varying degrees of success.[2]

The distinctions between action- and routine-seeking behaviour, and the different experiences which had resulted from it, were a particularly important aspect in parents' attitudes towards their children, especially in relation to crime and delinquency. Fathers in the action-seeking model had acquired street knowledge, attitudes, and justifications in their youth which differed little from those of their sons. Their portrayal of delinquent exploits were often romanticised so that offending seemed appealing and acceptable (as dad had done it). Mothers attempted to counter these images and discourage crime, as some examples from the younger generation of youths indicates. Dean, for example, told me:

> If there's trouble me mum tells me to walk away. Dad, I don't really talk to me dad much, he's out most of the time, I don't really know what me dad says.

None of the boys said that his father had made any attempt to stop them mixing with friends identified as trouble-makers. Mothers had. When they truanted from schools, fathers said they could not punish the child for something they had done themselves, often to mum's exasperation. When I asked John, one of the teenage youths, whether his parents had ever given him any advice about staying out of trouble, he said,

John: My mum told me last time [she] had to go up the police station, she said if I get in trouble again she won't come out, she won't come up to get me.

JF: Did that scare you?

John: Well if she doesn't come up to get me I don't get out. Me dad won't go up there.

JF: Why not?

John: I think there's a warrant out on him, cos he hasn't paid his fine.

Fathers therefore were viewed by the boys as rather weakly committed to disapproving of their behaviour and would often jump to their sons' defence (see Chapter 6). It was mothers who were most feared, as they did not share a similar viewpoint; Gary, for example, said it scared him if the police 'tell me mum' because she disapproved:

When I was on holiday with the school . . . I come back and give me mum all the presents I nicked for her and then I goes, 'Oh yeah, I got caught thieving' and she goes 'What!', and threw a cup at me.

The world of work

Although generational continuities in the women's experience and that of their mothers and grandmothers before them were marked, one aspect of their lives had altered dramatically in post-war years because of greater opportunities for employment outside the home (cf Nissel 1982). Although many women still worked as cleaners for necessity, others had secured predominantly white-collar work, which was a source of considerable enjoyment. Carol for example, although she had very young children (5 and 2), continued to work as a secretary. Her work was of central importance in her life:

I'm murder for work. I could be dead on me knees but I'd still go to work. Don't matter how ill I feel. I go to work now for the sheer reason that I don't like being at home.

Seven of the nine women in the darts team worked full time (excluding Joanne and Michelle) in clerical and secretarial posts. Their experience of work was very different from the physically demanding and unrewarding work of their husbands. In the search for 'embourgeoisement' (cf Zweig 1961) it is perhaps among women rather than men that attitudes are changing, since they were exposed to middle-class values and attitudes more consistently. Sal's attitudes for example were clearly influenced by her working environment, where the existence of career women who were educated and detached from the cult of romance and marriage reinforced and particularised her general belief in the importance of education. Chris shared a similar viewpoint. These two women were the only individuals in the study who did not support capital punishment and the efficacy of imprisonment. As Sal commented:

> I honestly think that half your prison population are the non-intelligent group of the London people or English people. People that are intelligent don't get in that kind of trouble. They might be frauds, work out a bank raid but they're not the type of guy who goes out there and does it. People that have got a good education behind 'em just don't get in that kind of trouble. I mean there probably are a few. I'm saying if you take a hundred people, probably eighty of 'em are working class and that's all there is to it. The solution to your problems is to educate 'em better.

Despite their recognition of the importance of education, Sal's and Chris's children were likely to replicate the experience of the parent generation. Chris's eldest son, for example, stopped going to school at the age of 14 and Chris herself had realistically low expectations for her children; she told me: 'I couldn't see any of my kids being a brain surgeon or lawyers or anythink like that: that's well out of their league.'

While work was clearly a source of satisfaction it also placed additional burdens on the women and (because of their exposure to differing values) raised their expectations. Some came to question the nature of their highly segregated role relationships. One of the few serious conversations I heard in the Grafton concerned just this issue. Chris told me that she would 'love to have an affair' and would like to be on her own without having to worry about domestic duties and responsibilities for a while. She said 'In eighteen years I have never been on me own . . . now I want to be on me own . . . I don't want to have to think about anyone else, about washing, cooking, housework, nothink.' Sal told her: 'If you didn't have anyone to worry about you'd have nothink.' Chris disagreed and complained that she was taken for granted by her family who never helped at home. Sal replied, 'That's the way you've brought 'em up – you haven't made 'em do things.

There is a wealth of survey data (cf Jowell and Witherspoon 1985, Mansfield and Collard 1988) which indicates that women do a large proportion, if not all, domestic tasks in the home. 'Real' work in working-class culture is regarded as hard physical graft; sitting down in an office was not considered work, and there was little, if any, recognition of the strains attached to trying to combine the roles of housewife, mother, and employee.

Differential socialisation

what characterizes the behaviour of most teenagers far more than their turbulence is their conformity, conformity to a patriarchal sexist society in which both sexes lose out. The boys who are prepared like boxers for a fight to earn their living, find a wife to provide them with a family, yet retain their sexual and social freedom; the girls, even today, are prepared for a life centred on domesticity and motherhood.

(Lees 1986: 155)

The routine-seeking behaviour of women and the action-seeking of men occurred largely because of the differential socialisation the two sexes received. Boys were encouraged in the action seeking model to be 'macho', tough, and aggressive. Girls, on the other hand, were expected to prepare for their future role as housewives and mothers. Their freedom was restricted and they were socialised into a more passive role, being encouraged to conform to authority rather than reject it. Joanne, for example, explained that Billy brought up their young son 'harder' because he 'needed it in the outside world.' Women, it was assumed, needed to be protected from that world.

The differing experiences of the two sexes was clear from early childhood. Boys were encouraged to enter into a 'cult of masculinity' (Willmott 1966) where fighting, sexual experience and toughness gained respect. Crime had an important role in this regard because it was seen as a pursuit which illustrated 'bottle' (courage) and won praise and esteem. Jimmy, for example, describes the response of his peers when he was released from borstal:

They seemed to think you was the bee's knees, 'Ohh mind out he's just come from inside'. Obviously you played on it.

If boys did not maintain this macho image they were considered 'poofy', or accused of being a 'mummy's boy' (cf Gans 1962, Young and Willmott, 1957) This was reinforced by parents at an early age and related to all forms of behaviour. Barry, for example, persistently referred to his son as 'poofy' simply because he refused to eat fish and he always encouraged the boy, who was shy and timid, to fight and stand up for himself. Jimmy, similarly, would scold his son, who was only 6, and call him a sissy. Many observers of working-class life have noted that the dominance of women in child-rearing and the vacillating presence of a male figure can result in a concern among adolescent boys about their sexuality (cf Miller 1958). Involvement in peer group activity and juvenile crime is seen as a 'solution' to such problems. Therefore, when Carol described her first husband, who had never been in trouble with the police, she argued:

Ed was very staid about anythink like that. I think it was his mum's doing more than his dad's. His mum used to smother him a bit, he was a bit of a mummy's boy. He was a right goody two shoes, he wouldn't believe in doing anythink that wasn't legal and above board.

The commission of criminal activities, therefore, contained elements of risk, danger, and excitement often identified in this culture with manliness (Miller 1958). When Carol described her life after meeting Jimmy, she said 'things got a bit livelier', much of which was due to Jimmy's activities.

Girls, on the other hand, were discouraged from toughness and had their freedoms restricted from an early age because of concern for their sexual reputation and because of the domestic duties many were expected to perform. Behaviour which was almost always praised in boys was strongly deterred in girls, as Chris illustrates in an account of a fight she was involved in as a teenager:

One time in the school holidays, there was a girl who'd I had a bit of contact with. We was queuing up to go in the swimming pool, and my mate Barbie turned round and said somethink to this girl. She started acting all flash in front of her mate. She was a hard nut and was known as a hard nut. She went over to Barbie and sort of started to slap her about. . . . I said, 'Look, you heard what she said, leave her alone' and she bashed me up. I ended up getting black and blue. . . . When I went home me mum done her nut. I don't even know how they found out where she lived, but we went round her house and me mum took me, and there I am standing there all black and blue and she said, 'Look what your daughter done to my Chris.'

These differing experiences of socialisation influenced women's participation in criminal subcultures, their experience of the education system and their aspirations and attitudes. These issues will be discussed below.

Girls and subcultures

Until relatively recently female crime has been a marginal concern for (mostly male) sociologists. As women account for a tiny proportion of the number of offenders overall, they have generally been neglected or described in highly stereotyped ways. Although an enthusiastic wave of research was inspired by the feminist movement and argued that female adolescent subcultures were becoming as violent and aggressive as their male counterparts (Adler 1975, Brown 1977) few British studies have supported these accounts (see Shacklady Smith 1978, Campbell 1981, Welsh 1981 as exceptions). Consequently more recent work has focused on female offending as an independent entity, where it is often the contrasts rather than the similarities with male offending which are regarded as most important.

McRobbie and Garber (1976) suggest that, since the enormous expansion of the teenage consumer market, one of the subcultural options available to young adolescent girls is a 'culture of the bedroom', where in the privacy of their own room young women can meet with their friends and play records away from the 'pressure' and 'ridicule' of their male counterparts.

The 'culture of the bedroom' in itself does not explain girls' marginality or lack of street presence because it is probably most prevalent among middle-class rather than working-class girls. None of the Grafton women for example had access to a 'bedroom culture', because most of them shared rooms as children (in some cases three or more to a room). The streets or areas close to the flats where they lived had always been their playgrounds, but the dynamics of their relationships were very different from those of their male peers.[3]

The substantial differences between the men's and women's juvenile experience was rooted in parental expectations. From an early age the women were expected to perform domestic chores and simply did not have the same opportunity to roam the neighbourhood and hang out on the streets. Carol, for example, the eldest of five children, said much of her youth was spent changing nappies:

> I was at home more than I was out . . . a lot of it was spent feeding this one and changing that one's bum and takin' this one up the shop in the pram. . . . I always used to do me own washing, I had to do me own room out. Right up till when I got married, Saturdays, I had to do the living room out and after Sunday dinner I had to wash up. If I hadn't done any of them things, I didn't go out: that was right up to when I got married.

Griffin (1982: 12) argued that these restraints crucially influenced women's 'schooling, leisure, and position in the labour market'. Lees (1986), Shaw (1978), and McRobbie (1978) all note similar trends in their accounts of young working-class women.

It was not merely during school years that the women were subject to restraints on their freedoms; even when they went to work they had curfews and were punished if they did not keep to them. The reasoning behind such measures was that they might get 'into trouble', although what exactly this meant was rarely explained to them. 'Trouble' was almost without exception seen in sexual terms.

One of the most interesting contrasts between the women's account of their adolescence and those of the men was the level of passivity they adopted in the face of parental and other authority. Sal and Chris, for example, said:

> We never questioned anythink. For example when I was gettin' married I had a double wedding with me older sister, the night before we wanted to go for a drink and my parents told me that I couldn't. They did not let me out the day before I was married and I never questioned it, you just accept that that's what they tell yer and that's what you done. . . . When I was at work, 16, 17, 18, before I left home I had to be in at 10 o'clock. Again I didn't like that, I resented it, but I done it. If Del and I wanted to go the pictures we either had to leave half way through to be home or we had to forewarn 'em and find out what time it finished and then they would time us, how long it would take to get home from the

pictures. That was right up 'til the time I got married. They was very strict.

(Chris)

My mum and dad never talked about the wrongs and the rights of the world, you just did what you were told. When I was 17, first boyfriend, I used to have to be in at 9 o'clock at night. If I was late, you know two minutes late I used to get walloped. He was pretty strict.

(Sal)

I mentioned at the beginning of this chapter that the mother–daughter relationship was very important and that women often expressed a wish to do what their mothers had done before them. However, this relationship was not without antagonism: the women's freedom was often infringed by their mothers, as Carol explains:

Me mum just grinned and beared it. She has well and truly been in a rut for years. She's always been a stop at home with five kids and that's it. Gradually the kids have got the better of her. She is literally as she says, a wash, cook, clean and that's it. That's how she looks at it. But I think me mum resented it a bit, the fact that she was indoors with the kids, cos they was all so young and that, and there was me out of a night. I mean if she was ill, it was always me who had to have time off work to look after her. So therefore I couldn't go out of a night. Sometimes she seemed to revel in that.

It seems therefore that from a very early age responsibility was instilled in the women. They were expected to perform domestic tasks and simply accepted this unquestioningly because of the role models set by their own and their peers' parents. Clearly these factors had an important impact on their opportunity to offend. This will be discussed later in the chapter. For the moment I want to focus on the women's experience of education and their attachment to the 'cult of romance'.

Education

Given the lack of emphasis on educational achievement in working-class culture in general, and assumptions about the women's future lives as housewives and mothers, few expectations were placed upon them to succeed. Unlike the men, the women's experience of school was largely passive. They neither truanted regularly nor worked energetically. They just passed the time until they could leave. Chris was the only exception. She rebelled from the last year of primary school until the third year of secondary education.

> I never joined in any activities and I never got on and done any school work whatsoever . . . the three of us were known as rebels, we had devilment. . . . We just didn't settle down. If there was a lesson, if the teacher wasn't a very good teacher and we could rib 'em, we would. The really weak teachers we used to give 'em a dog's life. I got slapped a couple of times by teachers. I got slung out of a music lesson, it was in an annex of the building and in the lobby of the annex was a whole board of light switches and I was playing with all the light switches and the whole of the school buildings were all having their lights turned on and off, on and off. . . . I never really disliked school, I think it was the fact that most teachers was rather boring. But when the third year came there was one teacher who I really admired and she pulled me to one side one day and she really gave me a pep talk. She said that I had the potential there and if I was to get on in the world I've gotta knuckle down and start doin' some work. What she said made a lot of sense to me. I think what it was, she was the first person who ever spoke to me as a person.

The importance of role models during socialisation cannot be over emphasised. In the case of the women these almost exclusively involved working in traditionally female occupations (cf Sharpe 1976). Chris, for example, had always wanted to be a secretary like her cousin, whilst Sal and Carol were also swayed in a similar direction. The boys, on the other hand, if they had role models at all, were more likely to mould their behaviour on the bad boys of anti-school culture than the college boys (Whyte 1943) or 'ear'oles' (Willis 1977). McRobbie and Garber are probably correct therefore in their belief that female cultures should be treated as separate and distinct from male ones. As Chris explained, despite her rebellion she always had a very strong sense of not wanting to 'do anything against her parents'.

> I would never do anythink wrong against me parents. I think that's what it was. I don't think I was really frightened of me parents but I just didn't want to let 'em down. I always didn't do it because I knew it was what my parents didn't want me to do. I didn't have the bottle for it. I think the biggest thing we ever done, I think we

nicked sweets off the counter once for dares at school. I hopped
the wag one afternoon and I was ill over that, never ever done it
again. When we was with the café lot we used to have the canal
and we used to climb over the bridges, go into the barges and just
used to take the barges up the canal, which we knew was wrong.
The wharf warehousemen used to come out and chase us. Once we
had the police chase us and we climbed up the bridge and got
away. But apart from that I can't remember doing anythink else
that was in any way connected to a criminal offence.

Life for the women in their youth therefore was not filled with the
creation of excitment or sporadic delinquent encounters like their male
counterparts. Asked to sum up their adolescence, Sal and Carol said:

> I used to go swimming twice a week. Home at half past nine or me
> dad would be walking the street looking for me. Then I started
> work we used to go down the pub. I used to stay in three nights of
> the week.
>
> (Sal)

> Boring. It really was. When you look back on it I never done
> anythink out of the ordinary or anythink really bad. It makes me
> wonder how I put up with meself sometimes. . . . I had to be in at
> a certain time, the dear soul that I married I met just before I was
> 16 and by the time I was 16 we was engaged so that more or less
> tied that up.
>
> (Carol)

Chris, on the other hand, while subject to the same restrictions on her
freedom, was also part of mainstream youth culture in her teenage years.
She had associations with bikers and a clique of mods whom she knew
through work. She joined many clubs, regularly went to the cafés, and
hung around with a crowd. None of these people was ever in trouble.

> We used to hang about in cafés and . . . I got to know the motor-
> bike boys, and although they weren't really rockers . . . they were
> still motor bike fanatics. They never got into trouble, they never
> had fights. If they knew that all the rockers were meeting at
> Southend to beat up the mods, they'd go to Brighton, they'd stay
> away from any trouble. We used to have weekends on the bikes,
> go racing at Brands Hatch. . . . [The crowd at work] they was very

cliquey, they were always out for a lot of good fun and again there was no crime whatsoever involved.

However, as Chris met Del and spent more time with him, she stopped seeing the bikers and clique.

Gradually we used to go out more together. We never used to go far, round his house or round my house or if it was nice and sunny we used to sit in the park, and go to the pictures, I think that was basically all we used to do.

Unlike the men, the transition from adolescence to adulthood was far more dramatic for the women and although they were as eager for adult status it took them down a very different path. The female friendships, which were very important in adolescence, declined at adulthood and any solidarity the women received through these friendships disintegrated as they became involved in relationships. Griffin (1984: 17) argued that 'This breakdown of female friendship groups undermined the basis of female cultures outside school and the workplace, and paved the way for [white] women's future isolation in the home as wives and mothers.[4]

The orientation to marriage and romance: reinforcing traditions

For most working-class young women, 'leisure' time outside the school and waged work does not offer many sources of 'thrills'.... The experience of 'romance' can serve to generate excitement ... day-dreaming about pop stars and boys passes the time in and out of school; gossiping about who's going out with whom and 'falling in love' can be a thrill and a source of shared excitement for these young women.

(Griffin 1982: 8)

Throughout early and late adolescence idealised notions of romantic love and marriage were the major preoccupation of the Grafton women; their attitudes wholly reinforced traditional feminine roles (McRobbie 1978, 1982, Griffin 1982, 1984, 1985, Lees 1986). As Lees (1986: 105) noted, 'girls through their relationships with boyfriends and their domestic responsibilities at home, realise that they are already having a taste of what marriage will be like'. Although the women often realised that the theory of romantic love and the actual reality of relationships differed substantially the vast majority remained committed to marriage and motherhood. Some embarked upon this path at a very young age because, in some cases, they felt pressured to conform, as Joanne explained: 'Marriage is a big thing to yer, all yer friends are gettin' married so you've gotta get married.' Others, however, took this path because it provided them with status; as Griffin argued, marriage is often the only sphere where women feel they can succeed and for this reason alone those who do not conform are considered abnormal, difficult to identify with, and perhaps threatening.[5]

Even where young women have broken free of these pressures and constraints and opted for subcultural involvement, in a gang for example (see Adler 1975, Brown 1977, Campbell 1984a), young women often end up reinforcing traditional roles and values which a cursory glance at their behaviour might overlook. As Campbell argued about young women's participation in New York gangs:

> Though the girls may buy the rhetoric of rebel and outlaw as a solution to their female identity problems they quickly find that street fights and robberies do not a rebellion make. In gangs, sex roles are not forgotten, for the subculture is embedded in traditional values, where women gain respect through fidelity, decency, and motherhood. If the girls themselves were ever to really doubt this, the boys of the gang would soon remind them.
>
> (Campbell 1984a: 311)

Present day attitudes and regrets

The women often felt when they looked back that their lives had been filled with missed opportunities and many of them regretted having married so early. Joanne, for example, said:

> Sometimes I do regret getting married and havin' the kids, I wouldn't part with 'em now but I wish I had done other things instead of it or not got married so soon.

Chris said if she had not had the children she would have left:

> If I had a way that I could plan me own life, I don't know whether I would have had the kids, cos I think if I didn't have the kids we probably still wouldn't be together. I think I would have had too much independence and I would have gone. . . . I had the opportunity of going, with the firm I worked for when I first left school, to Swindon. They was gonna get us the house and all that,

and he wouldn't go. It's always been the grass is greener on the other side, there's always been those would I, should I have?

Whilst Sal was categoric:

Go out and see life before you get married, before you get tied down with responsibility. Get your education ... get yourself a decent job, go and see a bit of life before you get tied down and get all that responsibility. Your life is never your own once you have kids. Never. It's somethink that I wouldn't change but it's somethink I wouldn't want [my kids] to do. I wouldn't want Tracey to come in and say at 17, 'I've met the man of my dreams, I'm gonna marry him tomorra', I'd really do my best to talk her out of that, or say live together for a year. I'm trying to get them to an age where they can take the responsibility a bit better than we ever did.

Despite such aspirations, underachievement in education and early marriage persisted.

Women's knowledge of crime: attitudes and rationalisations

it would be difficult to ascertain how far criminal values are endorsed and supported by working-class women in Fulham. Generally, the pub does not play such a central role in the women's social life, and consequently she has less access to the attitudes which circulate most readily in a pub environment. Furthermore, until recently at least, 'respectable' working-class women were particularly susceptible to the conformative pressures of a patriarchal society. . . . These pressures were presumably responsible for larger deferential patterns (in relations with the law, in attitudes to Royalty, etc), but it seems just as probable that communal loyalties would take pride of place over all other considerations at times of crisis (ie when a member of the family, or neighbour clashes with the law).

(Hebdige 1977: 19)

I illustrated earlier in the chapter that differing socialisation and constraints placed upon women during their childhood and teenage years led to their absence from street life. Crime did not form a major part of their activity and their knowledge of it was very limited. Sal, for example, reveals how her own perception of certain kinds of behaviour differs from Barry's, because she has never been involved in crime.

> If I actually saw a shop being robbed, I'd know that was really bad. But if I saw a gang of boys standing round a car, I'd just think it was a gang of boys standing round a car. Barry would think, they're gonna nick that car in five minutes time I wouldn't think of things like that.

Due to the traditional and highly segregated relationships between men and women in the Grafton, crime was rarely a topic of discussion in mixed company, either in youth or adulthood. Chris, for example, had had no knowledge of Del's juvenile activities: despite having known him for many months, it was not until he appeared in court that she found out:

> I knew he was hangin' around with a crowd that had sort of like been in trouble with the police before . . . [but] we never used to talk about it . . . I used to have to be in before them, I never used to know what happened after that.

Almost twenty years later very little had changed. Chris commented, 'I don't know the half of what he gets up to.'

Women's knowledge of criminal behaviour came from a number of factors which operated on different levels. First, as they were not perpetrators of crime their experience of it came either as victims or through associations with those who committed crime. At an abstract level the women recognised that crime was wrong and those who perpetrated it should be punished, but this abstract awareness was compromised by personal knowledge of, and involvement with, those who engaged in criminal activities. This resulted in a number of conflicts which involved issues of loyalty and practicalities. The women dealt with these dilemmas by distinguishing between their private awareness of a spouse's involvement in crime and the public recognition of it, in a similar manner to Sykes and Matza's (1957) techniques of neutralization. Chris provides an excellent example:

> I don't like anybody doin' anythink wrong and Del was obviously doin' somethink wrong. If Del wanted to stay with me then he'd have to change his ways, there was no way I was gonna stand for that. Although he still dabbled in his little bits, he didn't do anythink like breakin' and enterin' anymore.

Reducing Del's activities to 'little bits' ensured, at least publicly, that Chris could maintain Del had changed his ways: the reality of his situation would suggest that he had not. The fact that Chris did not know 'the half of what Del got up to' was functional both for her and for Del. In part her lack of knowledge of Del's activities allowed her the right to reserve judgement since she had only a partial picture of his activities. Had she realised the full extent of his dealings, such knowledge would have required her to reassess his behaviour.[6] The same dilemma was not posed once he had committed crimes and got away with them, as she indicates below:

> I never liked him doin' anythink dishonest, but once they've done it and got away with it, then I don't really know. It's difficult to say. I mean I wasn't the one to turn round and say 'Don't give me any of that money, because it's bad money, I don't wanna know'. I mean I spent it just as much as they did. . . I would never have said 'No' to anything . . . he's never been violent.

Chris's statement contains several rationalisations which are worthy of attention. The first is that the act itself is not deviant, only if it is so labelled by the process of getting caught. She justifies Del's behaviour by arguing that he's 'never been violent', illustrating her belief that some forms of crime are worse than others. Since she has accepted the fruits of his activities she must also exonerate herself – 'he wasn't doin' anythink *really bad* anyway'. 'Really bad' behaviour began at the point where Del's or any other husband's/boyfriend's involvement stopped. Chris also maintained, as I described in Chapter 2, that crime should not be so easy and that as Del stole only from people who 'could afford it', his crimes had minimal impact. Carol similarly argued that Jimmy had been an 'unlucky sod on the quiet really'.

These rationalizations served to cushion the women's abstract awareness that crime was wrong, as they also had to face the more problematic and practical difficulties incurred as a result of husbands' or boyfriends' behaviour. These difficulties ranged from personal dilemmas as a result of their failure to reform the men, to practical issues like dealing with the police and other agencies when husbands were arrested. Their reactions took several forms according to the stage of offending (ie juvenile, adult) its possible consequences, and the importance of the relationship. However, all the women's rationalisations concealed a deep sense of disappointment that their husbands continued to offend and bring additional stresses and difficulties into their family lives. Carol, like Chris, adopted a reforming role after her initial knowledge of Jimmy's activities, she said: 'You feel all virtuous . . . I shall keep him on the straight and narra', he will not stray from the path again – but he did!'

Failing to get men to conform to the law-abiding model, to which the women themselves subscribed, they needed to adopt a number of explanations and rationalizations to explain the behaviour of their spouses. This is where knowledge of criminal acts after the event became important. This was functional not only from the women's point of view, but also from the men's as it served to direct criticism away from them personally and was practical in dealings with law-enforcement agencies, as Del explained:

> Anythink against the law I never used to try and let her know about it. I'm a great believer if she don't know she can't get herself into trouble over me. The police will not believe that the woman doesn't know. They will not accept that. But if you ask any form of criminal, he doesn't want his wife to know, his wife can get him into too much trouble. They just won't accept it.

Barry had a similar attitude:

> If she don't know what I'm doin' she can't lie to anyone who comes to the door – simple as that and that's a ruling that goes right through the card. Their wives know they're thieves and they're out doin' it, but they don't know when or where, so they can't answer 'em [the police]. And that's rule number one if you're a thief or a villain you don't tell people what you're gonna do, you tell them after you've done it.[7]

Susan Smith (1986) argues that despite the existence of this philosophy, prisoners' wives often report being pressurized by the police, who use them as vehicles to obtain admissions from their husbands. The women in Grafton often felt that the police treated them harshly, especially as they themselves had done nothing wrong. Some like Carol felt they were treated as if guilty by association:

> Whenever Jimmy's been in any trouble, it's the way they've treated me who hasn't done anythink, they always seem to tar yer with the same brush – because he's done somethink you must have and I think that's completely wrong.

Carol had one particularly frightening experience when she was arrested by the police after Jimmy had stolen some expensive stereo equipment from work (see Chapter 3). Although Jimmy admitted to me that he had taken it, his account to Carol, which she describes below, illustrates both her willingness to believe that he was innocent and the distorted account which Jimmy told her.

> He worked for [company] at the time and they had this tape recorder which... [was] faulty. Well Jimmy is normally very good with anythink like that, he can fix it. The bloke who was in charge of the stores and equipment said to Jimmy, 'If you can take it home and fix it, fair enough.' So Jimmy brought it home. ... I said 'What's that?' 'It belongs to the firm, I'm gonna fix it.' I thought to meself then is he tellin' me the truth here or what, I thought it's a bit strange, but I never thought anymore about it. ... On Saturday morning Jimmy goes to work, knock at the door. I've turned round and opened the door and this copper's just barged his way in, plain clothes, with a warrant and searched the flat. Anything electrical they took down the numbers ... uniformed copper went off and checked 'em. Course he came up and said, 'Tape recorder, that's stolen.' I said 'No, it's not.' He said 'It's on our list of stolen property.' Now Jimmy always maintains (cos he didn't particularly get on with this guy at work) that this bloke let him take it home to repair it and then tipped off the police, because someone must have told 'em there was somethink here. Anyway, copper said 'I'm sorry, love, we're not satisfied with your story, we're gonna have to ask yer to come to the police station.' I was shaking. I went down there, this policewoman took me in a cell and stripped me, everythink. I thought, I don't like this. When they let me go I ran out of that police station, there was tears streaming down me face and I've gone straight to his sister's. [When I] told Jimmy what happened, he said 'Well I never phoned the police and told 'em to come round.' Me brovver in law said 'I wouldn't think you would, you smart arsed little bleeder, look at her, she's just been nicked for somethink she doesn't know nothink about.' He honestly couldn't understand why I was so upset.

Attitudes to the police were firmly influenced by the personal involvement of husbands and siblings, and once more indicated the relationship between attitudes and experience. Just as offenders developed a sense of injustice towards the police, so did the women, but in this context it extended beyond police maltreatment to include those who executed their duty in a polite and amiable manner. Carol serves as an excellent example. Prior to meeting Jimmy her attitude to the police had been neutral (despite her father's rather antagonistic attitudes), but her views later underwent a considerable transformation:

> Actually if I'm honest about it now, I'm like me dad, I wouldn't spit on a copper if he was on fire, I wouldn't spit on him to put him out. I wouldn't, cos some of 'em can be right cows. You don't realise it 'til you have dealings with 'em, I don't think.

Carol gave an example of one of Jimmy's many court appearances, which illustrates how she managed to evade the question of Jimmy's guilt and focus instead on the police role. The following extract clearly reveals the two levels of experience and the dilemmas which criminal behaviour in the family created.

> The two coppers came up that had nicked him, and they said, 'You all right mate?' I thought how can you stand there and be so friendly? One of them looked at me and said 'Why don't you take a seat with the baby, love' and all this. I thought what are you being so nice for, you could be depriving my kid of a father here. That must be the first time I felt any resentment towards 'em. I mean, I know it's not their fault and they're doing what they're paid to do, and it was more fool Jim for doin' it, you know. It was just bad luck that he got caught. That must be the first time I felt any real resentment against the police.

Chris told me:

> The police was regular, he already had a criminal record, his name was known to the nick they knew where we were living. Once yer face is known to 'em, they never leave yer alone. So they just used to come and knock at the door at all different times, could be early morning, late at night, just whenever, if there's a job been done in the area they just spun the flats and the villains that they knew until they found somethink. It was just their attitude more than anything else, they made you feel very resentful, like made yer feel as if they had a vendetta against yer. As much as you tried to prove that there was nothink there and you was good, goin' straight or whatever, they never believed yer.

Female crime

I have discussed throughout this chapter the differing factors which influence women's development through adolescence, their lack of involvement in crime and their routine-seeking rather than action-seeking behaviour. This final section discusses the nature and construction of female criminality, given women's differing socialisation and experience.

Although there have been attempts to show that female crime is on the increase and that offences more closely resemble those of men (cf Campbell 1981, Brown 1977, Adler 1975), such theories have been, in my view, rightly criticised (cf Box and Hale 1983) as it is the differences rather than the similarities between male and female offending which are most illuminating. Given that crime is related to opportunity (cf Mayhew *et al.* 1976, Heidensohn 1985, Clarke 1984) many women are simply not in a position to get involved in crime. As Heidensohn (1985: 174) aptly put it:

> burglary is rendered more difficult when one is encumbered with a twin-buggy and its contents; constant care of a demented geriatic is not a conducive situation in which to plan a bank robbery.

However, Heidensohn argues that it is not simply these 'external constraints' which inhibit women's criminal propensity, but other less overt forms of social control which 'operate *upon* women' in the home (with domestic violence), in public (because their freedom of movement is restrained by fear of crime), in the workplace, and in social policy.

Although none of the women in my research had been involved in crime, there was general agreement that some women did participate in crime, but specialised more, got caught less, and were less likely to persist. Although women are in general absent from predominantly male crimes, when they do offend they operate to an even greater extent in the 'private' and less visible crimes such as fraud and forgery. Del, for example, dealt with a female 'kiter' (cheque fraudster) at his yard, who visited him regularly. He told me:

> Kitin', that's the worst for girls. Cheques. If she got hold of your cheque card she'd be out. She used to come to me quite regularly. She used to have to pay about a hundred for a book which is two cheques, and if you've got ten or fifteen cheques in there at fifty pound it's quite a lot of money even if she got half of it. She would go out and she got me jeans and shoes, whatever I wanted. I just said I'll have that and off she'd go and back she'd come and I'll

give her half the value. But everytime she come she was frightened of getting caught and she knew what she was goin' back to, cos she'd done a lot of it [prison].

The discussion in this chapter has indicated that for the Grafton women, and probably many other working-class women too, their role remains a very traditional one. They have not been liberated from the home and the constraints placed upon them by their cultural heritage. With the worlds of men and women so clearly divided we would not expect to find many women operating in male criminal subcultures as they have neither the opportunity or access. Neither do they develop the attitudes 'favourable to the violation of laws' (Sutherland 1949) or the street experience which might lead them into it. In view of this fact, female crime must be the subject of separate enquiry, rather than a comparative and competitive component tagged on to theories of male criminality. Such a subject is worthy of more serious enquiry and discussion (cf Heidensohn 1985).

Summary

This chapter has described the women who frequented the Grafton Arms. It described their differing socialisation, the greater social controls placed upon them during adolescence and their orientation to the cult of romance and marriage. Their lives also, save in the area of employment, reveal generational continuity rather than change. This was largely due to the importance of the extended family in which women felt a strong tendency to do as their mothers had done before them. It was the women's responsibility to keep the family intact, it was they who organised gatherings and attempted to encourage routine-seeking behaviour, despite the often irresponsible action-seeking of men. Their attitudes towards crime and law enforcement have also been described and the way in which these were crucially influenced by the offending of spouses and siblings, and how knowledge of this led to the emergence of a complex series of rationalisations.

Notes

1   There is some evidence to suggest that as people grow older their relationships change. Townsend (1957), for example, found that as people reached retirement they grew closer to their spouses. One respondent told him: 'When people get old they cling together more. . . . You get to know one

another better.' This was reflected in Cliff and Edna (Chapter 2) who often held hands and were very affectionate towards each other. Ageing also seems to influence men's participation in household tasks (cf Jowell and Witherspoon 1985).

2   It is interesting that research on lower-class and working-class culture in countries far removed from the United Kingdom should reveal such remarkable similarities with the community I have described here. These similarities exist, I believe, because all such communities were located in deprived areas, where people's lives were concerned with very basic survival. Women realised the importance of family networks for support and recognised that mobility and advancement came from hard work rather than hedonism – they strove to emphasise this in bringing up their children.

3   This was illustrated by two young girls aged 9 and 11, who, I encountered during the youth part of the research. They sat on the steps of the block of flats playing banks, talking, and singing songs. This was in marked contrast to the behaviour of the boys, who spent much of their time being destructive, smashing bottles and windows, for example. Even in the older age group, the girls would sit and talk quietly amongst themselves about boys, clothes, and babies.

4   Griffin (1984: 17) argued that women 'in the same working class neighbour-hoods were least likely to lose touch'. The friendship between Sal and Chris pursued since school days is an obvious example of this. However, it could be suggested that the maintenance of this friendship was partly due to the close relationship between their husbands, which ensured continued contact.

5   I encountered this in my own research with the youth groups. One of the girls enquired whether I was a 'real woman' as I was 23 and unmarried.

6   This attitude is aptly illustrated by Violet Kray's comments about her sons, the Kray twins. She said, 'If they were involved in any trouble I didn't want to know. It only upset me. And as I knew that both of them was good boys at heart, I knew the things people said about them couldn't be true'. (Pearson, J. 1983: 47)

7   Taylor (1985: 162) notes that women were 'kept well out of everything while all went well but [acted] as alibi messenger and general fixer when trouble arrived. It was hardly an enviable position. They were unlikely to receive any great financial advantage from their husband's villainy: most of this money was spent on gambling and drink. Neither did they share any of the excitement of the escapades: all they saw of the action was limited to the traumas of early morning police raids, long and humiliating visits to police stations and jails, frantic efforts to raise money for bail and bribes, followed by prolonged imposed purdah which was the consequence of their husband's imprisonment.

Chapter five

Youth: like father like son

The previous three chapters have described the adult generation: the clientele of the Grafton Arms, the business which was conducted there, and the attitudes of both the men and women towards crime and law enforcement in general and in relation to their own offending in particular. The case studies in Chapter 3 illustrated important transitions from the 'public' sphere of crime in which Del, Jimmy, and Barry were engaged during their youth to the 'private', more institutionalised sphere during adulthood, where the opportunities presented by the occupational setting and extended family networks fulfilled the pursuit of 'easy money' with little risk of detection. Attitudes, however, remained the same.

This chapter focuses on the two contemporary groups of teenagers who were also subject to observation and interview. It describes the nature of their street experience and the contacts youths had with law-enforcement agencies in this context. Both were crucial to the formation of negative attitudes. The second part of the chapter concentrates on the preoccupations of the late adolescent stage, which precipitate a gradual transformation into the private sphere.

The kids on the corner: the 13–16-year-olds

At first glance Cohen's (1955) description of working-class youthful gangs as 'negativistic, malicious and non-utilitarian' seemed an apt description of the 13–16-year-old youths who hung out on the street corner off Gorer Lane (see Figure 1, p. 4). Constantly in search of excitement and thrills to alleviate boredom, their behaviour appeared destructive and anti-social, designed to inconvenience and outrage adult society. However, what initially appeared as rebellion in fact masked strong cultural continuities between the youth and parent generation (cf Cohen 1972, Parker 1974, Gill 1977, Mungham 1976).

Although the youngsters did not strongly identify with adult culture and operated for the most part independently of adults, their attitudes and experience tended to reinforce parental patterns. This was not simply a matter of 'cultural transmission' as I noted in Chapter 3, but the result of independent experiences, which tended to replicate those of the parent generation. The boys' attitudes towards education, crime, and street life differed little from those of their parents.

Although the cafés, canals, and bombsites (the playgrounds for Del's generation) had long since been replaced by huge impersonal council estates, the street corner remained an important focus of the contemporary youths' lives. Any evening of the week 'The Main Event' and his friends could be found sitting on their corner or roaming the immediate area in search of excitement. This was often found in acts of vandalism, fighting, thieving, and menacing local people, but was interspersed with long periods of boredom where the boys sat on the corner wall waiting for 'something to happen' (cf Corrigan 1979).

'The Main Event'

Similar to other studies of British juveniles (Downes 1966, Parker 1974) these youngsters were a group and not a gang. Although they had no leader, Gary (15), 'The Main Event', was the central focus of attention. What he lacked in physical agility he compensated for in daring, and his title was largely derived from this. The boys admired him for his 'front', thieving abilities and quick tongue, and often looked to him to 'liven things up'. Gary tended to organise and give orders, particularly on thieving expeditions. As Darren said, 'Gary gives us all the orders, tells us where and when.' While Gary argued:

> If there's gonna be trouble I say 'No, run' [or] when to fight and all that. When we go places I tell 'em 'wait out here', but we ain't got a leader like.

Gary was a persistent truanter and had been taken out of ordinary classes due to his disruptive behaviour and poor attendance. His ambition was to become a 'fly-pitcher' in the market, and his entrepreneurial activities, even at 15, were extensive.

John

John (15) was labelled 'Brains' by the group, as he went to a good school and was considered clever, an image which was heightened by his wearing glasses. Although John appeared quiet and innocent, he had an extensive juvenile record, which included breaking into factories and warehouses when he was 9, in addition to carrying offensive weapons and stealing from cars. His father was a scrap metal merchant, who like Del had criminal connections.

Darren

Darren (13) (who was nicknamed 'Romeo because of his success with the girls) spent much of his time 'hoppin' school' with Gary. His father ran a local pub a few hundred yards from the corner, which was frequented by several CID officers. Although Darren wanted to join the armed services he told me 'I don't think I'm brainy enough, I'll probably end up running a pub like me dad.'

Joe

Joe was Gary's cousin and had a cheeky and likeable disposition. Slight in build, he looked much younger than his 16 years, but was confident and self-assured. Joe aspired to be a printer and hoped to work with his father when his college course ended.

Neil

Neil (16), a trainee chef on a Youth Training Scheme, lived with his grandfather in a block of flats close to the corner. For most of his life he had lived a few miles from Gorer Lane, but went to live with his grandfather, because his natural mother was in a psychiatric hospital and his stepmother had beaten him. Perhaps because of his past, Neil was quiet and reticent and often more responsible than the other boys. He continued to attend his old school out of the area and had neither the street experience nor the recall to the same familial networks. His brother, who had been in a great deal of trouble, was the only person the boys knew who was unemployed.

With the exception of Neil, the boys were extremely image conscious and spent a great deal of money keeping 'in the pose'. This involved being fashionable and 'showing off' or 'posing' in one's clothes. They wore designer label knitwear, trainers, and jeans (one outfit would cost upwards of £150) as well as baggy jackets, which were ideal for hiding things they stole. It was the 'show' which was important, and on a Saturday afternoon, youngsters used to 'pose' along the High Street in their best clothes. Despite the expense the boys often appeared scruffy and were all, with the exception of Gary, thin and pale. Most of them carried weapons, usually knives.

A small group of girls, Sharon (13), Julie (16), and Kathy (14), also congregated near the corner. Although they had been involved with the boys (both platonically and sexually), the girls tended to remain aloof from them and went in pursuit of their own 'laughs'. This was partly due to their reticence about the boys' behaviour, as Sharon explained: 'The boys are evil sometimes, a bit fuckin' nutty.' This was particularly the case when they victimised elderly and defenceless people on the estate, as the girls thought this was cruel and went beyond the bounds of 'having a laugh'. The boys, on the other hand, considered the girls to be a 'fuckin' bit silly', and made continual remarks about their sexual reputation and appearance (cf Whyte 1943 Horowitz 1983, Lees 1986, Campbell 1984a, McRobbie 1978). The girls' position therefore was very marginal. Julie was, to my knowledge, the only girl who was involved in crime. She 'kept dog' (watch) for her brother, who was a 'fly-pitcher' in the market, and provided the boys with information about possible places to steal goods. Gary said: 'She works with her brother fly pitching. She's into a lot of things.'

The relationship between the young girls who hung out on the street and their male counterparts caused considerable difficulties for me. Although I made efforts to be friendly with the girls and sought interviews with them, they had great difficulty identifying with me (see Appendix). As a result the majority of my time was spent with the boys and the girls figure little in the discussion of this younger group.

Perceptions of the area: competition for space and identity

Fellows around here don't know what to do except within a radius of about 300 yards. . . . They come home from work, hang on the corner, go up to eat, back on the corner. . . . If they're not on the corner it's likely that the boys there will know where you can find them. Most of them stick to one corner.'

(Doc in Whyte's *Street Corner Society* 1943: 256)

The Main Event and his friends had a very defined sense of area, which extended from the corner through the myriad of concrete blocks and corridors of the estate to the boundaries of the park. As I argued in Chapter 1, the park (for both geographical and cultural reasons) formed an important dividing line between Gorer Lane and Stanton, because of the presence of a sizeable ethnic minority population resident on the other side.

The boys were highly sensitised to the territorial threats they perceived in the area and it was only on their 'manor', which comprised the corner and its immediate environs, that they felt really secure. This was partly due to the presence of older groups of teenagers, some of whom formed 'posses' (large gangs) and had territorial control of the main road (a corresponding group ruled on the side of the park). 'Nobody bothers the Stanton Posers, but no one beats the Gorer Roaders' they chanted. The posses and older teenage groups in the area made the boys feel small, as Darren told me: 'We're at the bottom type of thing. . . cos we're the youngest.'

Instability in the neighbourhood also arose from differing practices, and attitudes among some of the residents on the local estates. The widespread use and abuse of drugs, for example, was perceived as particularly threatening and in this regard the youths exhibited a strong degree of conservatism. Although they had experimented with 'smokes' (cannabis), they had steered clear of 'scag' (heroin) which was widely available on the estates.

Despite the threatening environment only a short distance away, on their corner, next to an old and dilapidated 1930s council estate, the boys felt very secure and had an intimate knowledge of the residents who lived there. Locals were divided into three categories: 'good' people, who were open and friendly towards the boys and did not complain about their behaviour ('Anyone that's good, we talk to 'em'); those they feared, who they knew 'to run from' because they were physically stronger, threatening, or unstable (for example one man on the estate, who was known to have a shot gun and was particularly volatile, the boys knew to avoid rather than provoke); and the potential victims, mostly elderly or inadequate people, who made easy targets as they tended to live alone, and had few if any community ties. The boys describe below the verbal and sometimes physical abuse they meted out to their victims:

We was on the corner and Stanley was walking down the road

with his wife and we were goin' 'Oi you old wanker, you cunt, your wife's an old slag'. He come over to us and goes 'I think you done it' to Gary and he goes to Neil 'And I think you done it an' all.' I think [Stanley] was gonna hit 'em right and since then he goes, 'I don't want no trouble, just leave me alone.' We goes 'Alright fair enough.' [He] got about twen'y yards away, 'Fuck off you old cunt'. Everytime we see him now we just try and kick him off the bike. The other night Tony was there and he had this little dog with him, Tony got a big brick and threw it at him.

Bertha was another of the boys' victims. In her late 60s, she had been menaced and obstructed, had had her door kicked in on several occasions, and was taken into hospital after a nervous breakdown, for which the boys felt partly responsible. When she finally managed to get a council transfer, they could not resist giving her a 'going away present' and set her door on fire, as they describe below:

> We set Bertha's door on fire. Wicked weren't it. . . . She was moving and we said we'd give her a present. She hates us [laughs]. She had to go into hospital cos of us once, had a nervous breakdown.

Blacks versus whites

Considerable tension existed between black and white youths in the area. The boys argued that black youths were responsible for a great deal of crime, particularly in East Stanton, which was seen to be synonomous with 'trouble'. These perceptions of troublesome black youths conveniently served to detract from the boys' own deviant behaviour, as white youth was clearly responsible for much of the crime in both Gorer Lane and Stanton, as Tables 5 and 6 indicate. Despite the boys' stereotyped images of the ethnic minorities, there is little doubt that offences such as 'mugging' were viewed as alien and unacceptable and introduced an element of instability (and increasing police presence) that was both threatening and inconvenient. Despite the fact that all the youths had attended racially mixed schools, the boys felt that black culture was dominant in the classroom, believed blacks outnumbered whites, and said that racial conflict was common. Nevertheless the boys did differentiate between black youths they knew personally, whose behaviour seemed to contradict their stereotypes, and others. Unfortunately these personal contacts did little to reduce their stereotyped images. As Joe told me:

If you grow up with 'em, you know 'em, you know what they're like, [but] if you see one walkin' down the street you say 'Yeah, he's done somethink', know what I mean.

Table 5 Juveniles taken to Gorer Lane Police Station April–May 1985

Racial classification	IC1 (White)		IC3 (Black)		Other (incl. E. European, Oriental etc.)	
Sex	M	F	M	F	M	F
Juveniles arrested	17	5	7	2	3	–
Juveniles charged	5	–	1	–	–	–
Total	27		10		3	

Table 6 Juveniles taken to Stanton Police Station April–May 1985

Racial Classification	IC1 (White)		IC3 (Black)		Other (incl. E. European, Oriental etc.)	
Sex	M	F	M	F	M	F
Juveniles arrested	42	16	21	6	6	
Juveniles charged	15	6	6	1	1	
Total	79		34		7	

Source: Gorer Lane and Stanton Prisoner at Station Records, Metropolitan Police.

These perceptions were shared by the parent generation and by the police themselves and highlight, as I noted in Chapter 1 the threats which league division three villainy posed to the indigenous population in the area. The Main Event and his friends argued that it was important to differentiate between 'honest villainy' (property crime) and crimes against the person, particularly mugging. Gary, for example, argued that he wouldn't get involved in 'drugs and mugging old grannies', whilst John said that he didn't 'mind "honest villainy" but when they go stabbin' people I think that's atrocious.'[1] These attitudes were strongly influenced by parental experience (cf chap 6). John's notion of honest villainy for example was derived from his father's 'business' contacts:

'I know 'em through me dad, he knows most of the villains'. These villains, like Del's, tended to be white property thieves.

Opportunity structures: pursuit of easy money

Those who have concentrated on the negativistic aspects of juvenile delinquency have often failed to see any rationality in juvenile behaviour. Indeed it is difficult to see in acts such as vandalism any utilitarian process. However, a proportion of the boys' time was spent in a highly rational manner engaging in the pursuit of easy money, which utilised local opportunity structures (cf Parker 1974, Gill 1977). These acts were 'rational' as it was the relationship between crime and 'gain' which was important. Just like Del's and Barry's escapades on the building sites, the boys wanted 'easy money' to spend.

For Gary and his friends, the close proximity of the market offered a ready opportunity structure for exploitation. Youngsters worked on the market stalls, observed the tricks of the trade, and gradually developed knowledge and connections. They stole clothing and other articles with ease and regularity. Although the boys' thieving tended to be opportunistic, local knowledge and networks were required to sell stolen goods. In an environment which thrived on the informal economy these opportunities and outlets were not difficult to find. Gary, for example, exhibited considerable entrepreneurial enterprise – 'I'm good at business, I always get money' – and, like Del, had a number of outlets which although much less sophisticated were sufficient for his needs. For example the caretaker's wife bought designer jumpers which he stole: 'Whenever I get good name jumpers, I always go to her. She gives me £8 for jumpers.' I asked Gary if she knew the goods were stolen; he told me: 'Everytime I go up there she says "You be careful, but if you get anymore bring it up."'

The Old Bill: the persistence of experience and attitude

The unstructured and public nature of the juvenile experience inevitably brings youths into contact with the police and these contacts are crucial to the formation of negative attitudes. The Main Event and his friends bitterly complained that the police persistently stopped them and treated them with suspicion. The incidents described below are typical:

One morning me and Darren were walkin' to school with our

gloves on, one of 'em came up to us and said 'There's been burglaries round this area, do you mind if I search yer?' and I'd just nicked all drinks and crisps out of the shop and he goes 'Did you pay for this?' and I goes 'Yeah'. He goes 'What shop?' and I goes 'That one over there, do you want to come over there?' and he goes 'No it's all right, we'll leave yer' and then just let us go.

(Gary)

He goes to us 'I've got to search yer cos you look suspicious for burglaries' (we both had gloves on) bleedin' shit 'in'it.

(Darren)

Joe recalled similar experiences:

When we used to hang about our estate, we never had nothink to do, [so] we used to stand around, laugh and joke. They [police] tried to do us for loiterin' and things like breach of the peace. . . trying to accuse us. Like the other day, [I] went down me cousin's house, I'd been down there about two minutes, [a] police car came roaming round the corner pulled up – we'd been sniffing butane gas, how can yer sniff that? I wouldn't, I wouldn't go within ten yards of the stuff. Anyway he tried to accuse us of all that. We goes 'Does it look like we've done it?' He goes 'Well you know, if you keep doin it, it'll kill yer within a week', and just got in his motor and drove off.

While Neil argued:

If you're walking down the road, they just pull you up and search yer . . .[for] knives or drugs.

Although the boys resented the attention they received from the police, they also gained an element of satisfaction from it because it gave them greater street credibility. As Welsh (1981) argues, 'police attention serves to confirm [kids] sense of group identity, autonomy and power.

In reality it was difficult to establish whether the Main Event and his friends were any more prominent to the police than other groups of youths in the area. However, the fact that they were frequently involved in delinquency had an important impact on their responses to being stopped and questioned by the police. With the knowledge that more often than not they had done something wrong, the boys often assumed that the police knew this too. Whilst on some occasions this may have been the case, on others it clearly was not. Willis's comments about the lads' visit to the headmaster in a Birmingham Comprehensive are especially apt in this regard:

> Whenever one of 'the lads' is called to see the head, his first problem is to mentally list the many things he might be interrogated about and his second problem is to construct a likely tale for all of them. When the formal and informal intersect, the guilt and confusion in his mind is much greater than the sharper sense of culpability in the head's mind. There is often real surprise at the trivial and marginal nature of the misdemeanour that has 'caused all the fuss' – especially in view of the hidden country which could have been uncovered.
>
> (Willis 1977: 32)

The disparity between the police's knowledge of the boys' behaviour and their actual involvement was a source of anxiety and excitement. The latter provided many hours of amusement and gave the boys the opportunity to 'get one over on the Old Bill' (a source of much satisfaction), as the following example illustrates. The boys had been riding in a stolen car, driven by Neil's brother. As the car careered out of control and hit a wall, they climbed out and ran back to the corner, about 200 yards from the wrecked vehicle. The police arrived and approached them. Back on their own 'manor', they told the officers a completely fictitious account of what had occurred, describing in detail the two black youths who had crashed the car and run off.

Although the youngsters enjoyed 'gettin' one over on the "Old Bill", they were in general, like the adults, fearful of authority and of the police in particular; more often than not they would run from, rather than confront, the police. This fear is well illustrated by Joe:

> If a policeman chased me I'll run. . . . cos policemen pick on anyone. . . . In school I done a project on law. I went to a police station interview and all things like that. You know I was really worried, I walked into the police station, I thought they was all gonna jump on me and take me in a cell for questioning and things like this.

This fear was partly confirmed by the youths' own experiences and those of their contemporaries and parents. John, for example, said:

> you get done for 'sus' or burglary, things like that. If someone's burgled, cos they know we hang round there, [and] we're the only

117

kids that really hang round the blocks, like if someone got burgled, he's gonna come straight to us.

Although the boys disliked and resented the police, as Welsh (1981: 265) commented, 'it is the way the police do their job, rather than the nature of the job they do which causes concern.' The boys' most bitter complaints were directed towards the young officers: John for example said, 'They're only doin' their job really, but like some of 'em, the young ones, they're the worst.' Neil said, 'young ones like they want to get promoted . . . and they pick on yer.'

Complaints about young police officers may have been so prevalent because, with the exception of home beats, young officers and probationers (who were inexperienced and under pressure to make arrests) were most likely to be doing routine foot patrols. Older officers did not experience the same difficulty asserting control over teenagers as their younger counterparts, as a local home beat officer explained:

> With a lot of the youngsters who police the streets now, when there's a stop done, it's not the policeman doing police work and the young kids maybe being asked questions, there's immediately a sort of confrontation – an abrasive attitude towards each other. Maybe it's a young man and a macho image. You know 'you want aggravation, you're Old Bill, I'll give it yer.' Unfortunately young policemen invariably take the same attitude, they haven't got enough experience with police work to talk their way out of things or talk people into listening to what they're tryin' to explain.

The boys' attitudes therefore strongly reflected those of the parent generation. However, unlike their elders, they had all managed to evade any form of custodial sentence and the police were often the only section of the criminal justice system to which they had been exposed. This was partly due to changing attitudes towards juvenile offenders, with the Children and Young Persons Act 1969, the creation of the Juvenile Bureau system (see Oliver 1973, 1978) and the introduction of cautioning (see Ditchfield 1976, Chapter 6). It was also due to the attitude of Gorer Lane officers' who sometimes felt that a firm talking to or 'chat' in the back of the car was a more effective method of dealing with juveniles than arresting them. This was not done simply for the youths' sakes, as juvenile arrests involved a great deal of paper work in addition to dealing with parents, and perhaps social workers and other agencies.

Officers' actions were also influenced by the nature of the area and their perceptions of the people who resided there. PCs often felt that summary justice was more appropriate than the 'formal' process of law, because the former was a language the youths could understand. By contrast, in Stanton, although many of these attitudes were equally prevalent, officers still used the formal procedures, so that although Gorer Lane had a higher incidence of crime (see Table 3) in most catagories almost three times as many juveniles were taken to Stanton (83 per cent as opposed to 17 per cent) during my observations with the police (see Tables 5 and 6).

John was the only youth in the younger group who had been taken to Gorer Lane (for possession of an offensive weapon and breaking into a factory). Darren and Gary had both been arrested several times but not in the Gorer Lane area. Gary was caught stealing on a school trip:

> I went on holiday with the school and me and my mate, we went in one of the changing rooms, where there's a swimming pool and we were nicking all the wallets, the watches, the lot. A couple of my other mates, they went round all the chalets smashin' windows and they got seen. Someone grassed me, so I got caught.

Learning to play the game: justifications and responses

I argued in Chapter 3 that contacts with law enforcement agencies during adolescence shaped attitudes, while getting caught led to the development of techniques of neutralization to explain deviant acts. Experience of and exposure to criminal justice agencies also familiarised delinquents with the processes and expectations of law-enforcement agencies. This knowledge led to a limited degree of negotiation and evasiveness on the offender's part, because once the juvenile realised what the accuser wished to hear, they could oblige. As Parker argues:

> To some extent the increased awareness of how the prosecution process works has helped the regulars take a small amount of evasive action. For instance it is wise when appearing before a magistrate to have just got a job: since the bench is usually aware of the employment difficulties of adolescents and feels some guilt about the situation, it brings some possibility of 'mercy'.
>
> (Parker 1974: 177)

Some of these techniques were noted in the adult generation and will be further illustrated in my discussion of the older teenagers. Among the younger group, Gary was the only youth who had appeared in court. The experience had left no lasting impression on him, but simply highlighted the importance of not getting caught again (cf Chapters 2 and 3). He told me:

> They just ask you all these questions. Did you take it, 'yeah' and then say all right 'That's the first thing you've done' (cos that's the first thing I done that I got caught on), 'You got a caution, let off this time, do it again and you'll have a criminal record.' If I don't get caught again then they'll scrap the record at 17, but I've been caught for other things.

All the boys employed several of the rationalisations outlined in Chapters 3 and 4 in explaining crime in general and their behaviour in particular. They saw their behaviour as quite natural and normal (cf Willmott 1966) and, like the adult group, saw crime as something that someone else did. Like generations of youths before them, that argued that they didn't go looking for trouble, but just found it. This was because street life was synonymous with trouble, particularly where differing groups were competing for territory.

The 17–19-year-olds: the intermediate stage

I argued in Chapter 3 that the transition from adolescence to adulthood was marked by movement from the public sphere of crime, inhabited by Gary and his friends whom I have just described, to the private and more institutionalised sphere in adulthood. This occurred because employment and preoccupations in later adolescence led to a decline in the frequency of offending and a partial withdrawal from street life. Contacts with law-enforcement agencies and the experience of getting caught also contributed to an evaluation of behaviour and combined, with access to work-related opportunities, to bring about a gradual transition into the private sphere. It is to a discussion of the intermediary stage between the public and private sphere and some of its characteristic elements which my analysis will now turn, in order to provide a fuller picture of the continuities in attitudes and experience of the two generations.

Although, as I pointed out in Chapter 3, the transition from school to work was not dramatic, there were important changes in later adolescence which influenced behaviour, if not attitudes. Parker (1974) noted a 'partial withdrawal' in late adolescence (17–19), as youths spent less time with their male peers and got involved in steady relationships with women. While this kind of withdrawal was evident among the youths I describe here, and had the appearance of conformity and 'settling down', such changes in orientation were in fact emphemeral when contrasted with the strength and persistence of cultural norms and expectations.

The 17–19 age group were friends of Tony, Del's eldest son. They were composed of a relatively small group of couples: Tony and his girlfriend Jane, Pete and Sandra, Terry and Karen, in addition to Andy, who was a friend of Pete.

Tony

Tony was the only male in the older teenage group who did not have a criminal record. He looked much younger than his 18 years and resembled his father in his slight appearance and quiet manner. Tony was a persistent truanter and did not attend school for most of the fourth and fifth years. He told me:

> I think what a lot of. . . gettin' out of school was that [with] me dad having a business, I thought I might be able to get on alright. I more or less knew I was gonna get a job with him and not goin' to school just didn't bovver me, cos I knew I could get a job afterwards.

After a brief and unsuccessful attempt on a government Youth Training Scheme at 16, Tony went to work for his father permanently. Although he had no convictions, he received considerable attention from the police, both while driving in the area, and working for his father. It is difficult to say whether this attention, which was sometimes as concentrated as four or more stops a week, was due to Del's activities, or simply because like other young men fitting the 'slag' category (cf Foster 1987, 1989), he was considered worth a stop.

Jane

Jane (17) originated from a very different background from the other youngsters in this group. Until the death of her father (when she was 11), Jane had lived with her lower-middle-class family in Wales. After her father's death, she refused to go to school and was eventually sent to a special unit as she was uncontrollable. When her mother moved to London, Jane still attended a special boarding school for difficult children, where there was no formal curriculum or examinations. She was an intelligent girl and enrolled on a government Youth Training Scheme (YTS) working with educationally subnormal children when she left school. Despite her love of the work, she refused to go to college on a day-release scheme and therefore had none of the necessary formal qualifications for employment after the scheme was completed.

Unemployed for a long period, she eventually found work, but was sacked for irregular attendance. Jane spent much of her time dreaming of marriage and babies and, shortly after the fieldwork, married Tony and had a child.

Pete

Pete (18) was a tall, blonde-haired boy, with an emaciated appearance. His dream was to join the Parachute Regiment but he had failed the entry tests on medical grounds. His mother was born in the area, and his father, who originated from Kent, worked in Saudi Arabia. Both sides of his family had a history of criminal careers. Pete told me,

> I think all me mum's side of the family have [been in trouble]. Her two brothers (my uncles), her dad (me grandad), everyone's been in trouble somewhere along the line. Johnny (me mum's brother) he's been inside about three times. I think one for assault, I can't remember the other ones, I think it was just theft and what have yer. But they've all been to court and DC, things like that. They've all been in trouble and they've all got a criminal record.

Although he always appeared charming Pete had a shadier and more violent side to him and often got involved in fights. He had done a range of jobs since leaving school (labouring, shop work, mechanic) and was employed as an electrician during the fieldwork period.

Sandra

Sandra had been seeing Pete for a year and a half, and was very possessive. She tried hard to steer him clear of trouble and tolerated bad treatment and abuse from him: 'I've not got much choice as far as Pete's concerned: if I don't like it, it's tough.' From the third year at school

Sandra 'hopped the wag', and although she secured a college place to train as a technician, turned it down, as she felt she 'didn't have the patience'. Instead she worked in a shoe shop in central London, which she disliked.

Terry

With a cocky and likeable disposition, Terry (18) was very much like Barry in the older generation. He had a tendency to be what the others called 'flash' and liked to be the centre of attention. Karen, his girlfriend, said of him:

> It's just that he wants to act flash. A criminal record to Terry is like being on 'This is your Life'. . . he likes to let people know he's got a criminal record, to him it makes him look big.

Terry's family had lived in the area for more than three generations and had always been in the 'fruit and veg' business. Terry argued: 'In that sort of trade not many of the people are straight: they're all like half villains.'

Like the others, Terry had a patchy educational career and was expelled from school for fighting. He took no exams because, like Tony, he believed he would not 'need 'em for fruit and veg'. But as he had to wait to inherit the shop, he sought alternative employment when he left school, again via family connections. His work record was sporadic. In the eight or so jobs he had gained since leaving school, he had held none for more than nine months, either because he was sacked, made redundant, or gave in his notice.

Karen

Karen was a quietly spoken pleasant girl, who dressed in expensive clothes. She was 'on the dole' for two years after leaving school but had supplemented her unemployment benefit by working for her father in his car accessory shop, and in a local shoe shop until she got a job as a dental nurse.

Karen had been engaged to Terry for some time and, although she recognised the futility of trying to change him, nevertheless spent a lot of time and energy trying. Her comments below are almost identical to the 'routine-seeking' behaviour (see Chapter 4) which the women in the older generation attempted to encourage, with equally little success.

I would like to concentrate my analysis of this older group on the preoccupations which existed in this late adolescent stage. The 'public' street existence played a relatively small part in the older group's lives. During the day they were legitimately employed, not 'hoppin' the wag' and roaming the streets like their younger counterparts. They were involved in steady relationships, which occupied more of their time, although it did not actually stop them offending. It was the new opportunities created by adult networks and employment which brought about a gradual transformation to the private sphere.

Relationships and marriage

The desire to assume full adult status in both employment and relationships is one of the major characteristics of this late adolescent stage, and is probably the only period when men and women spend a significant amount of time together. However, the restrictive nature of relationships, and the inheritance of firmly divided role models, led the attitudes and experiences of the parent generation to be strongly reinforced. Terry's attitudes towards marriage, for example, mirrored Jimmy's sentiments of twenty years before. Marriage offered adult status but there was little commitment or appreciation of the responsibilities (cf Liebow 1967). When I asked Terry whether he thought he was a little young to be considering marriage, he said

> Very young, think it's stupid really. That's between you and me, you can't tell Karen that. . . . I definitely wanna a kid [though] even if I have to get a council flat somewhere else.

The girls performed the domestic duties just as their mothers before them had done and tried to steer the boys clear of trouble by restricting their freedom and keeping them under close surveillance – something the boys resented.

> The blokes wanna go out and leave the girls at home and just go out somewhere on their own and muck about. We just wanna go out and do somethink silly, which the girls won't let us do, like Jane holds me back, Sandra holds Pete back, Karen holds Terry back.
>
> (Tony)

Sandra confirmed this. She told me 'I don't trust Pete with his mates:

they tend to get up to things'. Pete summed up the restrictive nature of his own relationship thus:

> I don't normally go out that often with Sandra, cos one, she normally has to be in by 11 o' clock on most nights, and if we go out and there's just me and her, or say me and my mates, which it normally is . . . she's very boring. I mean she won't drink anything more than Martini – she really does get the hump if I get drunk and she generally won't talk. So to me she's boring. I mean we can't go out on our own together, cos she'll either sit and watch me drink all night, or she'll just sit there and get the hump.

Given the restrictive nature of these relationship, one might ask why the boys did not simply abandon the girls. The answer lies in the fact that these relationships provided sexual gratification. Although instrumental, this was an important source of excitement for the boys, as Del explains when reflecting on this stage in his own development.

> I found that I could have much more fun without fighting, especially cos I knew what I was gonna get at the end of it! I must admit that I did find it better laying on the settee in the end.

Shover, in his interviews with ageing criminals, captures the meaning of many such relationships to the young offender. He wrote:

> Despite their involvements with women when they were younger, the interview subjects said that these were not important influences on their behaviour. Instead these were often exploitative relationships of convenience.
>
> (Shover, 1985: 93)

Although women did not have an important influence on the boys' behaviour, the desire for sexual gratification was partly responsible for the decline in peer activity in this age group, simply because they could not be in two places at once. However, there were also factors which made this decline in peer activity temporary. The first was that, once married, relationships became more predictable and restrictive, because the reality was very different from the expectation. This led men back to exclusively male domains, this time in the pub. Second, the boys, unlike their female counterparts, never abandoned their friends and the peer group remained important. They, like Del and his friends, simply waited until the girls went home to go in pursuit of easy money and excitement, as Tony describes in the incident below:

We got somethink to eat on the way home and sat down the garages at the end of my road. . . . We see a dumped Granada up the end of the road. It'd only been done that night, so they run down and started looking around. There was nothink left of it . . . the cops come round the corner and they just bawled us out. If there was something on it we would probably have got done for it, but there was nothing left on it to take. Pete and Andy ran off, Andy got away, Pete got caught and [they] pulled us back [to the station].

I will discuss this incident in more detail later, but for the moment I want to concentrate on how the boys perceived the changes in themselves in this period from early to late adolescence and the attitudes and explanations they attached to their behaviour.

Reflections on juvenile pasts

Although their street existence had only recently ended, Terry, Pete, and Tony were already involved in assessing their juvenile behaviour and actions. As they saw the generation below them doing the things they had once done themselves, such activities no longer held the same promise of excitement and adventure as they used to. Just like the older generation the experience of getting caught led to a reappraisal of activities. As Shover (1985) noted: 'Young adults develop the ability to see, to appreciate and to calculate more precisely some of the potential penalties that flow from criminal involvement.' This was reflected in Pete and Terry's experiences. Taking and driving away (TDA) was the major focus of these boys' activities in the 14-16-year period. Terry, Pete, and Andy had all been caught but only Terry received a punitive sentence (fourteen weeks at an attendance centre). Several themes recurred in the boys' explanations of why they had become involved in TDA: the influence of peers, the desire to drive, and boredom. Cars were symbols of masculinity and status, and offered excitement and the flow of adrenalin at fast speeds. This counteracted boredom. Terry describes how he got involved:

We just met a kid we know and we nicked a car and then I said 'I ain't gonna do it again'. Then one day they came round in a car and we went to Essex to see a friend we knew down there. On the way we nicked four other cars, one for each of us. I didn't know how to drive properly then and the car was going all over the road.

But I always had a love for cars, I'd always had a love for 'em. I just turned to TDA. Once I got nicked, I stopped I've never nicked another car since then.

Pete said:

I'd always liked cars, I love driving. I think it was a mixture between that and boredom, there was nothink really to do. Tommy, the bloke I used to hop school with, his cousin was always doin' it. Tommy started through his cousin and then I started goin' out with Tommy. It was mainly cos I like driving and because of the boredom that started it off.

Cars were the central focus of the boys' lives. They never walked anywhere they always drove. Many of their evenings were spent just driving round the area. As Pete told me:

We used to go out in the cars, not normally to a certain place, just like drive about. If we got to a long road [we'd] have a race, or [sometimes] go up McDonalds, the odd occasion the pictures or somethink like that.

Tony, to my knowledge, was not involved in TDA during these years, perhaps because through the breakers yard and stock-car racing (which was his father's hobby) he had access to vehicles without having to steal them. But cars also provided opportunities for easy money, because parts like wheels and radio cassettes were easy to steal and dispose of.

As I noted in Chapter 3 the experience of getting caught was an important one which had two results: it introduced an element of fear about the possible consequences of offending which hitherto had not been apparent, and led the offender to consider ways in which he/she might avoid detection in future. Pete's comments about taking and driving away illustrate his fears about getting caught and the risks involved. Yet, as I illustrated in Chapter 3, while these factors led to the adoption of differing methods, they did not bring about desistance from other forms of crime. Pete told me:

I'd never do it now. I mean I couldn't even if I needed to: I don't think I'd have the bottle to actually do it. I see the risks involved now, I see what can happen. The first time I was let off, the second time I was actually nicked for it. If I done anythink like that now I know I'd probably end up doin' time and I can't see the point in it anyway – it's just worthless. If I really got the urge to drive that much, I can always knock on Tony's house, he's always lending me the car. I see the risks involved now, I wouldn't do it.

Pete emphasised that this was a peer group shift and that his friends had come round to the same way of thinking.

> The majority of my friends that was doin' it at the same time as me, they've all come round to the same sort of conclusion. . . . No one hardly does anything now – like it's just pointless. I mean the main sort of crime I was gettin' into was TDA: most of us have got licences now.

Before one gets carried away with Pete's reformist wave, however, he continued in the interview to describe the 'silly' things he was involved in other than TDA, and despite an abstract awareness that such behaviour was risky and not worthwhile, these thoughts came only after the event. He continued:

> Ross, he had a [Ford] Escort, and *had* to get a spare wheel. He just took [stole] a spare wheel out of a boot. I would have been done for that. I was sat in the car, in the driving seat just in case he had to get away a bit quick. But apart from that there's nothing really been done. . . . I wouldn't do anythink now, even sort of sitting thinking [about the incident with Ross], I could see that it was stupid and if he got caught I would also have been done for theft. The risks are just silly now.

As I argued in Chapter 3, such statements are revealing not in their overt meaning, i.e. that he has learnt his lesson, but in the distance between intent and action. The reason Pete no longer 'joyrides' is because he now has legitimate access to a car; if he didn't he would still do it. Seeing the risks does not actually deter behaviour, as offenders do not believe they will get caught. As Karen said of Terry:

> If Pete . . . was to say to Terry, like the hospital's just closed down or somethink like that, we'll go down and get some plasters and sell 'em, we can get £30 out of it or somethink like that, Terry will do it, he don't stop and think 'No, I won't do it, I could get caught', he'd do it.

Just like Del and his friends, the pursuit of easy money was an important aspect of this group, where knowledge and networks were extremely important. Tony had a particular advantage because of his knowledge of the scrap trade and knew where to go for the most lucrative deals. Cars not only provided a source of excitement and income but also attracted a great deal of attention from the police. As Andy commented: 'Any young kid in a car under 20 they stop cos they think you've nicked it and they keep nickin' yer till they find somethink.'

Attitudes: formation to consolidation

With several years of street experience behind them, and the formation of attitudes and feelings of injustice, similar to those of the 13–16-year-olds described at the beginning of the chapter, 'trouble' remained an important element in these teenagers' lives. They had collected their own tales of mistreatment and, true to Sykes and Matza's (1957) techniques of neutralization, had developed a very definite sense of injustice, but one they accepted with resignation (cf Parker and Allerton 1962). However, they had also learned that although 'the law' was 'trouble', there were ways of getting round it. They knew the rules of the game and the way the system operated so that they could, for the most part, avoid weighty sanctions being taken against them.

Andy had been most fortunate in this regard. An extremely bright and astute young man, he had been caught three times in one week for TDA. On each occasion he had given a different name and knew how to deal with the visit from the juvenile bureau officer, telling her that he had a 'good home life and all that'. Andy had managed to get three cautions. It is well recognised that 'behaviour' and 'demeanour' (Piliavin and Briar 1964) are of vital importance in the police's decision whether to arrest or not; whether to caution or charge (Bennett 1979); and in decisions made by the courts. Some of the boys were able to 'keep their cool' and play the game (i.e. act in accordance with the expectations of law enforcers) better than others. Terry, for example, tended to lose his temper with the police, which did nothing to help him, as the following case indicates where he was stopped by them in his own car.

> I got nicked with Karen in my mini. . . . I never had a full licence, but the car was taxed, insured and everythink. I turned round the corner . . . and it screeched a bit. There happens to be two police walkin' down the middle of the road with torches. They pulled me over and my view to the police is that I don't like 'em, never have done. So he said, 'Can you get out of the car, please, and pass me the keys?' I said 'Certainly', I was trying to be nice and Karen

went 'Don't start'. He said 'Can I see your documents please?' and I said 'Yeah hang on' and I flung 'em at him. He said 'Is this your car?' I said 'Yep' and by then I was turning nasty. He said 'Could you come over here, madam', and he's took Karen away and that I didn't like. So I started swearing at him and I call ₁ him a varied amount of names and he said 'There's no need to be like this.' What I didn't know was that they was only gonna give me a verbal warning and let me off, but by this stage I was too wound up to calm down and I just give him everythink I had, just swore the lot and he give me a producer [form to produce driving documents at a police station].

Clearly Terry's attitude did not help his fate, but what this incident and others like it indicate is that it is the misfortune of getting caught and the contemplation of strategies which might have avoided it, rather than a focus on what they actually did, which is of paramount importance. Terry, in describing how he had gone to produce his licence at the police station, said he gave the officer all the documents and just as he was about to take them back, the constable noticed the licence was only provisional. Terry explained 'If I'd whipped 'em quick I could have been out.' Similar attitudes and instances were observed in encounters during my police research that illustrated both the sense of misfortune at having been caught and the rational negotiation with law-enforcement agencies when there was little choice (cf Foster 1987).

During this 17–19-year period therefore a consolidation of attitudes towards law-enforcement agencies occurred. Again it was derived from personal experience and not the hearsay of friends and family. As Pete argued:

Pete: The majority of [police], I don't like 'em. I just don't like 'em at all. You do get the odd few, I mean I've been pulled up and they've been really nice about it – but nine out of ten times they are right gits from my experience. The way they are, their manner, sarcasm, just everythink like that, they're right. They always find somethink wrong with you, that's why a lot of times, if I am legal and everythink is right, I love to get stopped by the police, cos I like seeing their face when they walk away and they can't do nothink.

JF   Is your opinion reinforced by what everybody else says about the police as well?

Pete: No, I mean my opinion is based on what I've seen. My mates, their opinion of 'em, they do match mine, so I mean it's sort of like extra proof. I mean the opinions, that I just give yer, is from my experience and what I've seen.

The experience of court

It was not until I attended the magistrates court with one of the youths that I realised the importance of the notion that it was getting caught rather than committing crime which was wrong, and the extent to which this pervaded both juvenile and adult thinking. Court is the stage where policy-makers believe offenders finally pay their debt to society, either in financial penalties or by imprisonment. However, even in court, some form of mimicry of the system and evasive action was achieved. As one police officer commented, 'You find an uncanny number of people have just found a job or are about to get married, when they appear in court', in the hope that the Bench might be sympathetic. Other methods such as the approach to fines were integrally related to attitudes towards crime and law enforcement, as Terry illustrates:

[The magistrate] said to me can I pay anythink at the court. I said 'You're jokin' ain't yer mate. I'm skint' I said, 'I don't work'. I did work but I didn't tell 'em cos it was best for me to get out of it like that – I got away with it.

Terry was the only person in this age group with whom I actually attended court. A warrant was issued for non-payment of fines and the description below illustrates many of the essential beliefs held by all generations towards law-enforcement agencies: particularly the importance of a good story; and their ultimate belief that there is nothing wrong with crime and no reason to pay for it:

Terry was very tense about his appearance in court and believed that they might 'put him away'. When I met him in the lobby, he seemed nervous and spoke rapidly, saying he had tried to pay £20 towards the fine that morning. He said he had just taken a job with Pete and had to work a week in hand. As a result he didn't have the money to pay all the fine but said he'd explain to the magistrate that he would settle it as soon as he was paid. Dressed in his scruffy work clothes, with spanners and pliers hanging from the belt of his jeans, Terry went into the witness box and explained to the magistrate why he had not paid the fine. He was given seven days' imprisonment suspended for a week as he had shown an ability to pay. The amount involved was £36. As we left Terry shouted 'Seven days in the slammer I won't do it.' He concentrated more on the threat of prison than on the payment of the fine. He defiantly told me that he had 'twenty quid' in his pocket but he 'wasn't gonna pay the bastards it'. We went to a café and Terry decided he wouldn't go back to work, but would find some way of getting the money. He said he was owed some from an off-licence job.

(Research Notes)

Essentially Terry accepted no responsibility for the fine whatsoever. His anti-authoritarian stance allowed him to concentrate on the magistrate's harshness in comparison with the relative leniency he had previously experienced. Rather than looking for ways to pay the fine for something that he had done wrong, he viewed the whole system as against him. It was as if he had had nothing to do with the proceedings taken against him, and made no reference to the actions which had caused the fines in the first place. This was not merely a matter of public posturing, but was intrinsically related to the way in which certain forms of crime and offending were viewed.

Some of these observations were further confirmed by another defendant who also came into the café. I asked him how he had fared. He received a £260 fine for driving without insurance which was to be paid in instalments of £5 a week. As he left he commented 'Course I didn't tell 'em about all the savings I've got'. This is central to an understanding of attitudes towards crime in all generations. Although there are clearly cases where people find it exceptionally difficult to pay the fines imposed, in others the money is more accessible than we might realise but offenders are not willing to use it to pay fines. As Terry told me, he wanted money 'to do things' and really couldn't afford to pay the court fines as well. Although he had access to the money this was *his* money, and therefore he would try and pay the fines in a manner which damaged him least (usually via more crime!). Although his wages were low, the situation would not change if he earned more, because he would never have had enough. As Karen noted:

Terry has got no evaluation of money at all. He's got more debts than what money he'll ever earn. Like in a week, his week's wages is taken, everytime he gets his wages, he owes his wages – so really he's working for nothink.

Once out of the formality of the courtroom and the heavy atmosphere of power invested in court officials, the experience, although frightening in its potential, quickly fades. Pete, for example, although fearful of a custodial sentence, when he received a fine and two endorsements on a licence he did not possess, described his experience of court as 'a slap on the wrist'. Although there was an element of bravado in such statements, it is worthwhile to refer back to Del's comments about the effectiveness of courts (see Chapter 3), where he noted that it is likely that any punishment delivered by a juvenile court will be no worse (and perhaps lighter) than the physical punishment offenders had already received from parents. Both Terry and his sister, for example, on separate occasions received beatings from their father. Terry when he was collected from a police cell, and his sister, Joanne, when she was caught driving in a stolen car with Pete. Terry told me 'I heard him outside [the cell] shouting at the Old Bill, and I thought he's gonna kill me. I come out and sat next to him, and [he] punched me straight on the chin.' While Pete said,

> They took [Joanne] to the Old Bill station. She wouldn't say who [it was], she said she didn't know me. Her dad come down and he had the hump about it, he beat her up and she started sayin' my name.

Given the immediacy of physical violence, it is understandable that the court's penalties in hindsight were often regarded as ineffectual. As I noted in Chapter 1, summary justice was a prominent feature of the area and was considered to contain an element of 'natural justice' which the law appeared to lack. It was also more meaningful and gratifying. Two examples illustrate how summary justice operated in the area and the way in which it received the backing of parents and the local community. Pete discovered that some of his brother's friends had assisted a local burglar by giving him information about people on their estate who were out at work during the day. He told me:

> Had it been my family [who were burgled] we would have got back, through like major violence. I don't mean to boast but my family is pretty big, they know people. They know that if I did find out that somebody had done that to my house, I would kill 'em, I'd do time for it. I really would sort of beat 'em up.

Terry conducted his own summary justice when his flat was burgled:

> I found out who did it and went round there. I see him on the
> balcony, lifted him up, and put a machete to his neck. He burgled
> my house and that's what he gets. Me dad said 'You should have
> hurt him'. I said 'No, he's learnt his lesson, he won't come back'.

While Terry's claims may appear outlandish, this sort of behaviour did
occur on the estates and was confirmed by the police and reports in the
local press. These notions of summary justice inevitably reflected
attitudes towards punishment which mirrored those of the parent
generation, the harder the better. As a police officer who ran mock
courts as part of the police programme in schools aptly described:

> Their idea of punishment is absolutely incredible, just short of
> hanging was usually the most acceptable thing. You would say
> 'Well don't you think that's a bit harsh?' Their response was 'Of
> course not, if they nick somethink, fancy stickin' their hands in my
> mum's shopping bag.' This is just not on you know. 'I'd cut their
> hands off.' We've all found this when you set up circumstances
> where they've found that either theirselves or somebody close to
> them is gonna become a victim or were victims, they wanted the
> hardest possible punishment.

This kind of approach was reflected in Karen's attitudes towards the
police, and was one often held by the police themselves, that summary
justice and violence were the only way of getting the message through.
She told me:

> Well I s'ppose [Terry's] attitude is that he hates the police. I
> s'ppose I do understand. I mean the police are hard on 'em if they
> get caught for anythink, but that is their job, and they should be a
> lot harder on 'em than what they are. They might get a kicking for
> doin' somethink, they might get beat up in the back of the van,
> that's the only way they're gonna learn.

This association with violence as the only feasible and effective
response was particularly important, as efforts were made to encourage
youngsters not to take the path of older peers and parents. They tended
to use coercion and force rather than talking to them. Barry, for
example, said he'd kill his son if he ever found out he was in trouble,
whilst Pete said that if he caught his brother he 'would bash him to a
pulp'.

Images of criminality: I wasn't really doin' anything bad

Like their younger counterparts, these older youths described the area as crime-ridden, but once again made important distinctions between certain kinds of crimes. 'Everyone's at it' was not simply a rationalisation but a more general comment on the area where they all knew people and incidents of crime, varying in degrees of seriousness. Tony, for example, said the people he used to hang around with had all 'done at least six months... some for cars, robberies and breaking houses and all that.

Whilst Pete's description below captures the attitude of the parent generation, their rationalisations and the essential divisions drawn between crimes against the person and those of property:

> Nearly ten out of ten people at sometime in their life will commit a crime. [The Train Robbery] that sort of crime, I would say good luck to 'em because it wasn't like they was stealing from a person. I mean if someone broke into your house and took your stuff, no, I just don't agree with that at all. I mean all right I know I did through cars, but I don't believe things that you've worked hard for and saved, I don't believe no one has the right to sort of go in and take that. I mean I can see how bad and how wrong I was with the cars. But in the case of the Train Robbers, it's not an actual individual person. I mean that is like a load of people or a company, where all right I know the Train Robbery was a lot, but like theft in companies or whatever, is not really missed by one certain person that they get that much of a loss. . . . Housebreaking and burglars, they're, I dunno, that sort of person I class as scum, I class it as a completely different type of crime.

Notice how close Pete's view is to that of Barry in Chapter 3; as was Terry's description of mugging:

> I think that's disgusting. All they pick on is old people, unless like there's gangs of people, and they hit young girls and snatch their chains. Like we had a wave of stabbing fags out on babies' faces . . . round our way, now it's all calmed down, but it's still bad – I dunno what to bring it down to – bad upbringing, that's what I put it as. As I say, I've been in trouble meself but there's no need to go stabbin' someone for it. If you ain't got it you go without, that's the way I see it. If I ain't got somethink I won't go and kill someone for it, nothink like that.

Once more the distinction between words and deeds is important here. While Terry is probably right that he would neither mug or kill someone, his assertion that 'If you ain't got it you go without' is not an accurate reflection of his behaviour, as his search for immediate gratification and the details of his own attitude towards money have revealed.

The techniques of neutralisation employed by these teenagers also reflected the adult generation, both in the minimisation of activities, reduced to 'little bits' or 'silly things' for a laugh, and contained a ready catalogue of injustices to explain their behaviour. Again they emphasised the distinction between the occasions where they got caught, and those they got away with. Terry, for example, argued:

> I drove a bike for seventeen weeks with no tax, no insurance, no MOT, and no licence and got away with it. I know it's wrong but I *had* to do it. I was working . . . and I had to get there somehow. . . . Things like that I've got away with, but unfortunately I've been very unlucky in all, I've had to pay for it. You could say what I've paid in fines and that I've covered for when I've skipped road tax and things like that – so really I've been middle of the road. I ain't been too bad for me.

Pete, like Del and Barry, focused on the fact that he had not really hurt anyone, and possessed his own code:

> I've never thieved off any person. I mean if I was sittin' here I wouldn't take somethink off yer shelves. That sort of crime, no, cos I believe once a thief, always a thief. I mean I know I did with the cars, but I think as I said most of it was being bored.

The girls in their rationalizations adopted the minimalist approach that the boys' behaviour was 'silly' or that peer group influence drew them into trouble. Karen argued:

> I think most of the boys his age, who live round in my area, the ones that I know, have all been in trouble with TDA and silly things like that. I mean Terry's always been very easily led: if someone says 'Oh come and do this, come on, do that' he'll do it.

As I illustrated in Chapter 4, the perpetuation of such images as 'being easily led' was a functional but not necessarily correct assessment of the situation. However, such interpretations served to minimise and deflect blame away from the offender. Sandra similarly made three important rationalisations in her comments about Pete and his propensity to get involved in illegal behaviour. She told me: 'If it was somethink silly and he thought he could really get to it easy, he'd do it, just to help his mate out or somethink.'

Public to private

The intermediate years, owing to preoccupations with relationships, the assumption of adult status, and the new opportunities afforded by work, were characterised by a gradual shift away from the public sphere. These changes did not involve a stake in conformity or herald the beginning of a law-abiding life, but acted as a temporary inhibiter in the 'public' arena and combined with new outlets and opportunities, for the transition into the private sphere. Attitudes were by this point firmly established. Nevertheless there was some genuine reflection on the earlier teenage years and some assessment of risk, which also made the private sphere more appealing, since the hidden economy was not regarded as crime at all. Although this intermediate period marked the transition from public to private, it was not characterised by the low degree of risk which Del and others had achieved by their late 30s, as teenagers in late adolescence continued to be a major focus of attention for law-enforcement agencies.

From their new vantage point, Pete and his friends could cast their eye on their younger counterparts (who were still in the totally public sphere) and saw them moving inexorably in the same direction as they themselves had done. They offered advice, but as with those who had tried to deter them, such advice fell on deaf ears (cf Shover 1985). As Darren told me:

> Like the kid I call me brother, he tells you things he used to do and tells yer it ain't worth doin' it, cos it ain't got him nowhere, when he's done it. Like he tries to tell us not to do it and all this but [we] don't listen to him.

Pete described how he could see his brother getting into exactly the same kinds of trouble he had:

> I can see him how I was when I started doin' TDA. I'm pretty sure he's already started breakin' into cars for cassettes and things like that, cos he's always got car keys, and from what I've ever known the only reason you carry all these keys, is to either take the car, or get into it to take something from it. . . . I can see now why I

137

was like it, [but] he can't see the risks involved. He might be lucky and not get caught and then in a couple of years he'll sort of realise and stop like I have. . . I told him he's stupid, I mean it's just not worth it, but I was told that as well by friends when I was his age and I didn't see it, I took no notice, he'll probably do the same.

Although activities differed, attitudes remained the same. Still guided by the principle of 'easy money', Terry, Tony, and Pete had little need of the public street crime which characterised the younger group, as they were beginning to build their own networks where they assisted each other in 'fiddles', and work 'on the side' – things which were not considered crimes at all when compared with their earlier, more visible activities. Stealing parts from cars, goods from work, and acting as intermediaries storing or selling stolen goods, were examples of the common everyday 'duckin' and divin'' which was part of the adult world in Gorer Lane. On the day I attended court with Terry, for example, he had done a deal with Tony to tow away a vehicle for £50, had money due from an 'off-licence job', and still went elsewhere to find the money for his fine! Tony, in the garage and yard, had ready access to certain goods, and the knowledge and networks to sell them, as did Pete in the electrical trade. Such practices, like those described in the Grafton, simply became an unquestioned and normal part of their lives.

Summary

This chapter, along with the descriptions in Chapters 3, 4, and 5, reveals the marked generational continuities in attitudes among both the youth and parent generation. Like their fathers before them, street experience resulted in confrontations with the police and the emergence of antagonistic attitudes towards them. Contacts with law-enforcement agencies also resulted in the need to explain their behaviour, which led to the development of rationalisations to neutralise and minimise it. Youths acquired a rudimentary knowledge of the rules of interaction with law-enforcement agencies, while understanding these rules allowed them a small measure of control in their interactions. The period after leaving school was characterised by a high turnover of employment, but due to the extended family structure the occupational pool had not run dry. Fitting the 'slag' catagory held by the police, teenagers in late adolescence continued to receive attention from law-enforcement agencies. However, despite having been arrested on several occasions, none had to date received an adult conviction. This was due partly to their current preoccupations with relationships and the world of work, which led to a decrease in the frequency of offending, while employment afforded safer opportunities for the pursuit of easy money.

Notes

1   Although the boys behaviour towards Bertha may seem to contradict their statement, to them 'mugging' was a cold-blooded violent assault which was premeditated and done for financial gain. They on the other hand were 'having a laugh' and fighting boredom. Although this was a convenient rationalisation it does not of course detract from the moral repugnance of their actions.

Chapter six

Generations: past and future

The preceding chapters have described the attitudes and experiences of two generations in one area of South East London. This concluding chapter summarises the major themes which have been raised and is divided into four sections. The first briefly describes the nature of change in the national context from the 1960s to the present day. It describes the way 'youth' was treated as a distinct and separate phenomenon that influenced the focus of research in post-war years, and clouded the crucial importance of continuities in generational experience. The second deals with aspects of generational persistence in attitude, where the past experiences of Del and his contemporaries in both education and offending are used to illustrate how parents, particularly fathers, unwittingly provide the necessary assumptions and context for similar experiences in the next generation. The third returns to the question of punishment and its relationship to behaviour. The picture, as I have illustrated throughout, remains one of continuity rather than change. With this in mind, the final section considers ways in which we might intervene to prevent the repetition of attitudes and experience in subsequent generations.

The nature of change

The period between the mid-1960s and the present day has been one of tremendous social and economic change. As I mentioned in the introduction, the 1960s were dominated by theories which emphasised the emergence of a 'new' and distinct generation of youth. Hall and Jefferson argue that these images involved assumptions:

> that what happened to 'youth' in this period is radically and

qualitatively different from anything that had happened before. It suggests that all the things which youth got into in this period was more significant than the different kinds of youth groups, or the differences in their social class composition. It sustains certain ideological interpretations – e.g. that age and generation mattered most, or that youth culture was 'incipiently classless', even that 'youth' had itself become a class.

(Hall and Jefferson 1976: 15)

Many of these attitudes were given credence by relative increases in affluence, consumer consumption, and full employment among the working classes during the 1960s.

Since youth was regarded as a 'distinct' and 'new phenomenon', great emphasis was placed on 'youth culture' and the meaning of 'style' and their role in rebellion and differentiation from the parent generation. Isolating 'style' as the symbol of youth, however, concealed important continuities (cf Mungham 1976) in structural relationships, opportunities, and attitude. As Chris argued: 'In my day, it was the mods and the rockers, then the skinheads and punks, now it's the poseurs.' Yet as Gill (1977) wisely comments, these different youth styles are not indicative of a 'generation gap' or a cause of concern for the parent generation because while crazes like the skinheads, teds, or mods come and go the experience of different generations remains very similar.[1]

Although these images of youth with 'too much time and money' were not always accurate reflections of the areas where youth cultures often thrived (cf Pearson, G. 1983), the relative position of many working- class youths in Britain is far worse today than it was twenty years ago. Serious economic decline in the 1970s transformed the hope and optimism of the 1960s into a decade of fatalism and depression (Cashmore 1984), with high rates of youth unemployment, instability, dissatisfaction, and urban unrest (cf Benyon 1984, Scarman 1981: 6.28). Despite recent economic revival there is a generation of both white and black working-class youth who have never worked.

While such descriptions are undoubtedly an accurate reflection of the national situation (and formed the basis of expectations for findings in this research) the evidence presented here is clearly at variance with many of these trends. In fact an officer's assessment that Gorer Lane police were living in a 'time warp' is a rather apt metaphor for much of this research. The extended family structure regarded as a dying institution remained important; employment, a scarce commodity in many inner city areas, was available to the teenage generation; attitudes toward crime and offending were consistent with well-established, documented, and entrenched working-class attitudes towards authority (Miller 1958); while the way of life and relationships retained many 'traditional' characteristics. Such features, described at length in the preceding chapters, reveal the strength and persistence of working-class culture and raise important questions as to why and how it has been maintained.

The first elements, in what in many ways is a remarkable insularity, have been due to geographic and cultural isolation (cf Stedman-Jones 1971, Williams 1949), where, largely unhindered by outside interference, the culture has reproduced itself. Historically South London has always been regarded as 'the poor relation across the river' (Williams 1949). Although in the first instance its insularity was determined by the lack of communication links with the city, the availability of local employment, which burgeoned as a result of the industrial revolution, reinforced this pattern. In terms of crime, I described how the area had perennially been viewed as one of 'ancient ill-repute' and continues to be identified in a similar manner today. The people described here were in many ways akin to the costers in the nineteenth century, whom Chesney (1970) described as being 'out of joint with the times', yet both generations managed to survive and in some cases thrive on the informal economy, just as the costers had once done.

While there are important historical reasons for insularity and cultural isolation, I want to focus on the more recent past and discuss the consequences of theories which prevailed in the 1960s and the 'foreshortened historical dimension' which they adopted. Many of the popular theories in this period were influenced by an optimistic belief in a classless society (Zweig 1961) and an age of affluence for all. Research therefore compared pre-war and post-war conditions and saw change at every turn (Hall and Jefferson 1976). While it cannot be denied that post-war developments in the Welfare State, National Health Service, and other policy initiatives brought about qualitative change, this was always relative, and did little to alter or eradicate the major divisions in British society (Hall and Jefferson 1976, Mungham 1976, Townsend 1979). Similarly, although there has been an absolute shrinkage in the numbers of the working class and an expansion in the white-collar sector, relatively, the working classes, were, as they always had been, at the bottom of the pile. Ownership of a washing machine and stereo did not constitute a middle-class way of life (cf Goldthorpe *et al.*, 1969).

These differing influences, the one indicating material change, the other continuity, can be seen in the differences between the descriptions of the older generation's youth and those of the present day. Contemporary teenagers were seen to have greater material comfort, better housing, less discipline in the home, and more money. As Chris told me:

> There's more things about for kids now. If they want to go to a club, there's a club at the end of the street, whereas, there wasn't so much for us. It's much easier for them to have an education. There's a lot more electronic things around for them; computers, video games. They've got their own record players and even their own tellies in their bedrooms now. Most kids have their own bedrooms, whereas before we used to have to share bedrooms. It was unheard of that you had your own room. Most kids have got gardens, or spaces. They wouldn't know what it was like to be hungry and not have any money, or live with rats or the bugs. So I think kids have got it different today, but there again, I think every generation does. I've got it different when I was a kid from what my parents did and they were different when they were kids from what their parents went through.

Despite the belief that contemporary teenagers had a better quality of life, with more material possessions (just as they themselves were regarded by their parent generation) it was recognised that structurally things had changed very little. Barry, for example, said:

> Nothink's really changed in general. The basic facts are still there, it's just that things have progressed a little bit better. If they wasn't around [video and stereo], you'd be stuck with the radio like our parents had.

While Sal commented:

> Money was short then and it's short now. There was places to go when we was young, but you couldn't afford to go to the [youth] club every night cos you couldn't afford the entrance. That's all it is nowadays, is money. 30p to get into the club, 20p to play pool, you're looking at a pound note before they go anywhere. It's so expensive.

Although some descriptions of the past were tinged with a certain nostalgia and tendency to romanticise, particularly in relation to changes in crime (cf Pearson, G. 1983), there was nevertheless a strong element of similarity in their accounts. As Sal and Chris describe:

> As you get older you constantly hear old people say, 'It ain't like it used to be in the old days, we had terrific fun in the old days, we enjoyed this and we enjoyed that. We never had nothink, but you enjoyed your life.' And I think as I get older, I feel the same. I think if I had the choice, to be born in this age or my age, I think I would still have had what I had. Cos I've enjoyed my years; but then I think if you asked anybody of whatever age, they would always tell yer, I would prefer to be born when I was.
>
> (Chris)

> I can remember my mum and dad nattering to the neighbours next door and saying, 'Oh this is wrong, and that is wrong.' It's probably the same as we hear, people arguing about politics, and money, probably the same as they were twenty years ago. I mean he's [their son] enjoying his life, alright he'd like a bit more than he's gettin' but all of us thought that as kids.
>
> (Sal)

Although there were qualitative differences in the lives of the two generations then in terms of better housing, more material comforts and less punishment, such changes were superficial compared with the similarity of experience.

Attitudes towards children: disadvantage through generations

In searching for the roots of persistence and similarity in generational experience, the role of parental attitudes and educational experience are of paramount importance. As I have stressed throughout, the similarity of experience was not due to direct 'cultural transmission' (cf Liebow 1967) but resulted from subtle parental processes particularly in the father–son relationship.

Although Del and his contemporaries had not achieved in education themselves, they nevertheless wanted their children to succeed. They all recognised that academic success could provide valuable opportunities, particularly in the present economic climate where youngsters could no longer be guaranteed a job, especially without any qualifications. Yet the only couples with children beyond school leaving age (Del and Chris and Vera and Arthur) had reinforced parental experiences and there was little to indicate that siblings and contemporaries would fare any better. Although the extended family network often supplied employment for children, this was not always regarded as an ideal situation, because it did not offer the opportunity of 'betterment' which qualifications might achieve. Mothers in the 'routine-seeking' model placed particular emphasis on this, while fathers argued that education was the only means by which their sons could avoid 'ending up like them'. As Barry said about his own son:

> I hope that he goes straight and that he goes into college and gets somethink behind him. Not like me. I've told him there's no way he goes into the building game unless he works for hisself or he's the guvnor. That's the only way he can earn the money these days, apart from thieving it.

If we look at Barry's comments closely we find that, although they reveal a general desire for his son to do well, there were several factors, some more obvious than others, which influenced his son's opportunities and development. The first concerned the level of aspirations and expectations. These tended to be very restricted. It was commonly hoped that sons would work in 'a trade' (cf Goldthorpe *et al.* 1969), or be a 'guvnor'. Clearly many of these trades and traditional apprenticeships were becoming obsolete, while the opportunities to be self-employed were restricted to very small numbers. Although the persistence and entrepreneurial force of the culture had allowed some, like Del, to achieve a living outside the mainstream economy, changes in the area had begun to make this avenue less secure.[2] Second, while parents realised the importance of education at a theoretical level, they felt they could do little practically to help their children (cf Douglas *et al* 1968, Goldthorpe *et al* 1969)

It was not only parental aspirations or practical assistance that influenced the success of the older generation's children. There was also a conflict of attitudes in the men as a result of their own experience of the education system. As they had 'hopped the wag' because school was 'boring' and held little value for them, they were adamant that they could not punish their own children for doing the same thing. Jimmy, for example, said:

> I'd teach him hopefully the right and the wrong way. If they want to learn the hard way, there's sod all I can do about it. I can't condemn them for things that I've already done.

This, in conjunction with other endemic cultural factors which derided the value of education, obviously had important consequences for the way that schooling and issues related to it were dealt with, particularly by fathers. In some cases parental experience and attitudes could and did have a detrimental effect on the child's chances of success.

'Like father like son'

The accounts of hoppin' the wag and the general attitude towards schooling described in Chapter 3 revealed that Del and his contemporaries spent more time out of, than in, school. The same was true of the younger generations. As juveniles, Del, Jimmy, and Barry had developed anti-authoritarian attitudes which were recognised by teachers at an early age (Douglas *et al.* 1968, West and Farrington 1977, West 1982). Such attitudes were clearly visible in adulthood too and were a key factor in producing disadvantage for the next generation, as Barry's description of the school selection procedure employed both for him and his son indicates

> When you transfer [from primary to secondary] you apply to different schools. I applied to [name of school] but I didn't get in. They had a system that you had to know so much about Maths, Geography etc. The geezer (headmaster) asked me where the Isle of Wight was. I said 'I haven't got a clue.' He said, 'Well, there's a globe, go and find it.' [I replied] 'I'm not interested in finding it – you tell me where it is and I will remember.' That's why I didn't get in. They refused me, they reckoned I was argumentative – I mean how can yer tell in one hour?[3]

Barry then compared his own experience with that of his son's:

> I think the way they should go about it is to ask the parents what school they would like the child to go to. . . . Like Lee, we applied for a school and he come out with a grade one pass in his primary school. We went to the interview with him and the headmaster, or whoever he was, was interviewing me. I think [there was] a possibility that he thought well 'Like father, like son.' He said, 'Well, what do yer reckon?' and I said, 'Well look at his grades, that speaks for itself. You're the teacher, you tell me.' He said 'We like to ask the parents.' So I said 'I'm not applying for the school, he is. If you accept him, it's up to me whether I'm gonna let him

come here or not. That's the difference.' I don't think he enjoyed that neither and I think that's one of the reasons he [didn't get in]. They sort of put that power over you. They say 'I'm the headmaster and I've got the right to say yes or no.' But if they don't like me that poor little sod suffers.

Lee (13) ended up attending what Sal described as a 'grotty school', but, unlike his father, had managed to stay on the right side of the school gates, as far as they were aware. This was probably due to Sal's influence. She tried to temper Barry's behaviour and minimise the damage he caused, as she could clearly see its deleterious effects. She closely supervised Lee and prevented him from going to places she regarded as likely trouble spots, like the local football ground (cf Wilson 1975, 1980).

The same was not the case for Del's and Chris's eldest son, Tony, however, who did not attend school for much of the fourth year and most of the fifth. Del's response to Tony's 'hoppin' the wag' (which they discovered accidentally) was that he 'could hardly say anythink to the boy when he had done it himself.' Although Chris was worried and upset, Del refused to force Tony to go to school, but told him, 'Look how I've turned out because I've had no education: don't you wanna do better than me ?' As we have seen, in terms of this South London community, Del had done very well for himself (albeit on the wrong side of the law), which made his advice appear rather confusing and contradictory. Second, Tony knew that he could secure employment with his father when he left school and argued that this influenced and neutralised much of the advice about youngsters' needing qualifications to get work. Similar attitudes were expressed by Terry, Darren, and John, as they too had self-employed fathers and expected to get work automatically at 16. Tony did not attend school at all in the last six months of the fifth year. The authorities never contacted Del or Chris about his absence, and Del decided that Tony should work in the yard 'rather than walk the streets'. At 16, therefore, Chris argued 'Tony's got no qualifications, and no education. He can't even write a letter.'

This was a very typical account and reveals how disadvantage may pass from parents to children. Lipset's comments on the authoritarian personality reveal that poor education is a key factor in the expression of authoritarian attitudes. He argues:

Low education, low participation in political or voluntary organiz- ations of any type; little reading; isolated occupations, economic insecurity and authoritarian family patterns, are some of the most important factors contributing to authoritarian predispositions. Education in particular is the single variable most closely associated with such attitudes and with racial and religious bigotry.

(Lipset 1960:100–1, 476)

There was only one account which differed from the kinds of educational experiences described above, which involved Carol's brother, Eddie. Without help or encouragement, Eddie was able to read and write and understand other languages before he even went to school. Carol's witty account of her brother's talents reveals the enormous distance between the values and expectations of her world and that of the middle class.

Me dad was never one for takin' him to football matches and things like that, he'd go up the pub with dad and sit outside. But Eddie's always been very quiet, he was a bit of an egg head. At 4 years old he used to tell people how a radio worked. It got quite frightening at one time. He could read before he went to school and nobody had taught him. We found out purely by accident one morning, [when] dad was sittin' there reading the paper, 'studying form', as he put it! Eddie just happened to get up on the chair and look over his shoulder and he's said 'Here yer are dad, that one.' So dad said, 'Which one?' Eddie said, 'That one, Red Alligator.' Dad looked and sure enough it says, 'Red Alligator'. So dad sat there all morning with the paper opening it and pointing out various words and he read each one. So of course, me dad, not to be out done, went and got the dictionary and opened it, and it don't matter what word me dad picked out, Eddie could read it. Dad couldn't get over this. Of course it got to the stage where I s'ppose Dad goes in the pub and tells his mates, the word gets round, no one believes him. So he had all his mates coming home, 'Go on, you pick that dictionary up, pick any word you like and he'll tell yer what it is.' Course they done all that and Eddie read 'em and they decided to do it the other way round, tell him the words and get him to spell it and he did. It really did get frightening, one dinner time they had a Welsh programme on [television] and it was as though he understood every word they said.

Eddie became head of a department in a large German bank. He had no university education and no attempt was made to place him in a school for gifted children. This reflects the general attitude to education, as his ability was regarded as no more than a novelty and his potential was not considered any further.

Generational persistence in attitude

parental attitudes to juvenile crime, and their influence upon their sons, are more complex matters deserving special attention.

(Willmott 1966: 153)

Parental attitudes have rarely been the focus of research in crime and delinquency. As I noted in the Introduction, there has been an underlying assumption in literature on juvenile delinquency that its very expression represents a rebellion and rejection of adult values and parental attitudes. What we know from previous research tells us that parents do not condone delinquent behaviour but little attempt has been made beyond this to identify whether in fact parental attitudes differ from those of their delinquent children. Parker, for example, sees the conflict of attitudes between parents, peer group, and street culture. He wrote:

pressures of . . . large family, the lack of facilities and obsolete architecture, all push the energetic child out of parental control. Once out and about, parental words are often not a strong enough deterrent for the street-corner boy. . . . he is subjected to other versions of what is right and wrong behaviour. Parental views are only one standpoint; the youngster mixes also with the peer group and the men on the Corner. He learns to adapt his beliefs and behaviour to his company.

(Parker 1974: 43)

While Parker is undoubtedly right that juveniles learn to 'adapt' their behaviour according to their 'company', he assumes that parental attitudes are in opposition to those of their children. This may not be the case because, while parents do not encourage delinquency overtly and hope their children will 'go straight', underlying and rather subtle processes, particularly in the father–son relationship, actually reinforce the young adolescents' experiences.

Father's youth and activities

Among the males in both generations, all fathers had experienced some contact with law-enforcement agencies, either as juveniles or as both juveniles and adults. For the purposes of this discussion I want to concentrate on the younger group of 13–16-year-olds as they were, at the time of the research, most aware of their parents attitudes and expectations. In addition, I will use two incidents which involved Del and his son Tony, to illustrate how some of the more general principles of the father–son interaction operated in practice.

Although, as I have clearly stated, parents had no desire to see their children become involved in crime (cf West and Farrington 1977) parental experience unwittingly provided the circumstances whereby this became possible. In the adult generation, all parents said that they had told, or would tell, their children (according to their age) about their involvement in crime. As Del argued:

> I've never hidden the fact that I've been locked up. I've let them
> know that I've been locked up and I've let them know that I didn't
> like it. That's what I try to impress upon 'em more than anythink,
> is that I've been there and it's not a nice place to go.

This advice given by fathers to their children may at first glance illustrate that parents did not condone crime and contained the message that crime didn't pay. However, if we look at Del's comments more closely, it is not crime which is regarded as wrong, it is getting caught. His statement relates only to 'being locked up', not to the commission of crime itself. He more than anyone should realise that the fear of getting caught is no deterrent where the pursuit of easy money is concerned.

Second, one might be forgiven for thinking that crime did pay in his case, and that his continued and successful manipulation of business interests (which Tony was fully aware of since he had worked in two of Del's businesses) proved this. Crime, therefore, was an illegitimate avenue to success and status, as Cloward and Ohlin's (1960) theory suggested. This did not result from a direct apprenticeship, the internalization of middle-class goals, or status frustration, but from strong cultural traditions in the working-class context. The semi-legitimate 'sub-world', so aptly phrased by Hebdige (1977) as 'somewhere between the underworld and the surface', offered infinite variety and access for the pursuit of 'easy money'.

Crime also held a certain aura and provided periods of excitement and autonomy in lives which were otherwise very routine and boring. With their policy of openness about previous involvement in crime, fathers described their juvenile experiences in accounts which were often romanticised (not in terms of the harsh penalties, but in the fun and excitement of their actual execution). This made incidents appear more exciting than they probably were, so that delinquency became appealing and acceptable (as dad had done it). Women tried to discourage men from talking about their experiences for just these reasons. One of Shover's (1985: 69) respondents noted this dilemma and tried to avoid discussing his criminal career as he did not want to 'appear "unfatherly", or say anything that conceivably would appear to condone or to glamorize crime.'

The presence of deviant images also occurred at a time when there was a preoccupation with masculine identity, where delinquent subcultures based on 'toughness' provided an important avenue of expression for teenage anxieties (Miller 1958, Patrick 1973, Boyle 1977). Joe's description of his father's youth illustrates both these 'focal concerns' (Miller 1958) and the romanticisation of accounts:

Me dad was a villain. I think he was about 9 and he went to a new primary school. All the kids [tried] him out, so he beat up this kid and broke four fingers. He was only 9 and from that day on he never had trouble. Like everyone in the family knew how he grew up, like his sisters and things like that, all frightened of him cos they knew he wouldn't take no rubbish. Like if a kid wanted to fight him, he'd fight him no matter how many there were. But I think all dads are like that, dads fight, like now, they're grown up they'll fight for the interests of their son, they ain't gonna let their son get done by ten kids.

These experiences, which were passed down from father to son, also contained the catalogue of injustices which fathers had experienced in their youth, with rationalisations and explanations perpetuating negative images of authority (particularly towards law-enforcement agencies), and the use of alternative methods such as summary justice. As Joe indicates below:

Me dad don't like the police all that much cos, like when me and me brother get pulled up, it's for somethink stupid like writing on the wall, playin' football where you're not allowed to play football, things like that. [One night] it was about one o' clock in the morning, a man ([who] was drunk or somethink) was kickin' down our door. Me old man went out there and give him a right doing over. He was giving him body punches so like it wouldn't show, so me dad wouldn't get done.

John argued that his father had similar attitudes towards the police:

He don't mind the old ones but he hates the young ones. He's told me most of the things about the young ones, like when he used to be in the car they always used to pull him up when he was ridin' the motorbike, like Barry got pulled up. They just pull you up for silly things.

While Gary said of his father's attitudes towards the police:

Gary: My dad don't like 'em.
JF: What does he say about them?
Gary: Bastards.
JF: Why, has he had experience of them himself?
Gary: Yeah, like he got pulled up in his car; silly things when he used to break into factories. He don't like 'em. . . . He goes 'When I was a kid I done it all.'

In the extracts above we can see the 'minimisation' of offences to 'silly things', similar to others described at length in relation to business in the Grafton. It was not that riding motorcycles under age and without the correct documentation was a serious offence, it was rather that parents, by confirming these experiences, served to reinforce the boys' feelings that the 'Old Bill' were stupid and picked on them for 'silly things', rather than on the fact that they should not have been doing it. None of the fathers made any attempt to divorce their sons from the peer group or encourage them not to mix with 'trouble-makers'.[4]

West (1982: 49) argues that 'Poor supervision could be one of the most important ways in which parents fail to protect their sons from delinquency', while Harriet Wilson (1980) has reported that parents who were lax in their supervision of children were more likely to have delinquent offspring, particularly if they lived in areas with high delinquency rates.

Delinquency was often regarded by both generations as simply a product or hazard of living in the area which parents could do little about. Fathers in particular adopted a seemingly abstract concern for their children, where they theoretically wished to see them legitimately employed and law-abiding, but accepted their delinquency with an almost fatalistic inevitability if it occurred. As Jimmy describes:

> Me dad always said to me, 'You can learn two ways, the easy way or the hard way.' I've learned most of it the hard way. I'll try and get my boy to learn it the easy way, given half the chance. If they want to to learn the hard way, there's sod all I can do about it. I can't condemn him for things that I've already done. Cos they'll know what I've done when they're older.

Gans noted a similar attitude:

> When a boy reaches the age of 10 to 12 ... parents feel that he is now responsible for his own actions. If he gets into 'trouble' either police or priest, the blame must be attached to the influence of bad companions. Having done their best by urging him to follow home-rules, parents hope that he will do so. Should he fail to do so however, the consequences are ascribed fatalistically to his peer group and his own moral failings. But whereas parents are concerned about the results, they neither feel the same responsibility for the child that is found in the middle-class family, nor develop the same guilt feelings should he get into trouble.
>
> (Gans 1962: 58)

Gans's account is useful in explaining the relationship between parents and their children, particularly in the fatalistic acceptance of delinquent behaviour and lack of parental responsibility in this. However, in terms of attitudes and their relation to behaviour, it was the fathers' refusal to condemn delinquency which was the most important factor. Since the delinquent boys of yesterday did not discard their attitudes, but continued to justify and build upon them in adulthood, as fathers they shared certain common assumptions and experiences with their sons. Such experiences facilitated a form of collusion between father and son, in both knowledge of, and dealing with, law-enforcement agencies. When Gans describes parents blaming the peer group, this was just one of a number of rationalizations that were related to 'playing the game'. Since fathers had had similar experiences, they too had convenient explanations which could be used in their sons' defence, as the following discussion indicates.

The presentation of a credible story

> Roundhouse is in practice a 'condoning community' as regards its
> general attitude towards most kinds of delinquency.... The
> hatred of Authority is implanted at all age levels. In their own way
> parents and sons feel the same way and protect each other against
> officialdom.
>
> (Parker (1974: 190))

I have illustrated throughout that the South London community of Del
and his contemporaries and those of the teenage generation was a
condoning one. This is vitally important in understanding interaction
with and attitudes towards law-enforcement agencies, where both
fathers and sons attempted to formulate and present a credible story,
which justified action, and afforded protection and evasion from official
sanctions.

The assumption of innocence on the part of parents about their
children's activities arose for several reasons. The first was due to
purely personal factors, where parents refused to accept that their child
had committed the offences he or she was accused of. The second
concerned an estimation of the likely 'truth' of the incident based on
their own knowledge and experiences of being detained by the police,
and perhaps 'fitted up.' Therefore they did not automatically accept the
legitimacy of the police's account. Third, the construction of a credible
story produced a version of events thought suitable for the listener,
rather than an accurate account of what had occurred. I am unsure how
conscious these practices were, but the consequence was that both
juveniles and adults had only limited knowledge of the actual events.
The boys' accounts of their fathers' antics were sketchy and, in turn,
parents' knowledge of their children's activities often came to light only
when they were apprehended. As a result, sons related their accounts in
a form which played down their own involvement, as they had no wish
to implicate themselves and invite further trouble. It was easier for them
to claim that they 'hadn't done it' and were wrongly accused than to
admit their guilt.

Many of these processes are illustrated by an incident which occurred
during the fieldwork, when Del's son Tony was arrested (as a result of a
routine stop) for having a forged tax disc on his car. Del's account of the
incident highlights several processes in the construction and
maintenance of a credible story:

one of the guys that does bits and pieces for me, I asked him to go down to the post office and tax the car. I gave him the money, the MOT and all the paperwork to go with it. When the car came back, the tax was in the winda, I didn't think no more of it, until Tony got stopped. It was stolen. Even when I said to the copper 'How did you know it was stolen?' he said, 'Well, you'd never know, but I know.' I said 'Well, how was I s'pposed to know it was stolen?' You're banged up for three hours, you sort of sit there and think how the bloody hell does he know it's stolen? It turn[ed] out that the guy I had sent knew someone that was selling tax discs. I gave him £90, if he can go out and get one at 40 quid and get away with it, good luck to him. But it just happens it went the wrong way round. We were both locked up, Tony had about four and a half hours and I had three.

Before we proceed to the second stage of Del's description of the incident, it would be useful to consider some of his comments. First, given the nature of Del's dealings, it is certainly feasible that he sent the man to buy a disc for £40. As we saw in detail in Chapter 2, Del's whole business depended on keeping a credible front and he knew how to respond to questioning. In relating the incident to me, he adopted the same technique, as it was automatic to build in his 'self-exculpatory statements' (West 1982). It was, in reality, unlikely that he was an innocent 'victim'.

Second, his curiosity about how the officer knew that the disc was stolen indicates that Del may have known the disc's origins, but thought it had appeared legitimate enough to avoid detection. As his perception had been challenged, he wanted to know (perhaps for future reference) how they had known this. Allerton's description of the feelings he experienced on arrest give support for this assumption. He told Parker: 'I think the first thing's annoyance – with myself. How could I be so stupid as to get nicked? What's gone wrong, what have I forgotten, where have I made the mistake?' (Parker and Allerton 1962: 149).

Third, Del's casual attitude to the man who was responsible for his being 'banged up' did not accurately describe his feelings, even if he had known the disc was stolen. The man had 'taken liberties' and Del would seek retribution. This was a personal matter, however, not one for the police, as the rest of the extract indicates:

JF: Did they ask you to name the person who had gone off with the money?

Del: Yeah.

JF: Did you name him?

Del: No, it's a code, ain't it. I mean I did know who went and got it and where I could get hold of him, but it's a matter of making a story in your mind and sticking to it. I gave a name, the first thing off me head. I said I know roughly where he lives, let me go and find out. Then it's just a matter of give them as much bluff as you can. When I came away [released] the first thing I done was found someone on the Stanton estate that was squattin' about the time it'd happened. I gave that joker's address, yeah there was a squatter here and that's the end of the matter. I can't help it if he's gone, so it's a matter of hangin' on to that. But if I had got hold of him, I would have given him a right dig. The police would probably have given him two or three months p'rhaps. My punishment would have been a lot harder than two or three months, he'd probably do that standin' on his head. With me he'd have to do it standin' on his head. I don't feel I was holding anythink up, but just a matter of stickin' to what you say, cos the worst bit is once you start to lie, there's fifty other lies to come on top of it, and if you haven't got a very good memory, you'll get done.

Parker describes a similar presentation of a credible story occurring between delinquent youth and their lawyers. He argued:

The Boys tend to provide false information to their defence counsel. On one level they simply don't trust their gowned, wigged, and unlikely ally. On another they find it more economical to keep to one story of what happened from the beginning to the end of the whole affair. Hence everybody involved in the bureaucratic prosecution process is told the same story. At times The Boys hardly distinguish between the truth and their defence story themselves so that in a pub conversation they might actually find themselves practising their story of innocence to people that know better.

                (Parker 1974: 175)

With their own experiences, rationalisations, and explanations for behaviour firmly embedded, fathers approached instances of their sons' delinquency with a ready catalogue of injustices, and responded according to these rather than on the evidence presented to them. This is illustrated by an example mentioned in Chapter 5, where Tony was arrested with Pete and accused of stripping a car. Del immediately leapt to his son's defence, proclaiming his innocence without once trying to establish whether in fact Tony had committed the offence or not. This seemed to be irrelevant. Instead, regardless of guilt, it became a question of '*us*' against '*them*' where aspects of 'playing the game' were required for his defence with stock responses for those in authority. A police officer at Stanton with nearly twenty years' experience told me that both in his duties and his role in an attendance centre he observed just this kind of behaviour. He said:

> They answer you in the stock way for the stock questions, as somebody that's in an authoritarian position. . . . Speaking to kids and juveniles, even in the presence of their parents' you'll find that dad will answer, and you can tell whether he's villainous or devious cos he will answer in a way that he thinks that you ought to be answered in. It really is following that particular evasive pattern.
>
> (Police Constable, Stanton)

Techniques of neutralisation (Sykes and Matza 1957) were also required, which explained and reduced the culpability of actions. This involved finding an acceptable explanation, albeit an inaccurate account of the proceedings. Del adopted the argument that his son would never tamper with cars, as he had ready access to them in both the yard and garage, and that Pete was a 'trouble-maker' and bad influence on him. However, as we have seen, Tony openly admitted that he would have stripped the vehicle if any parts had been left. Either Del did not know this was Tony's attitude, chose to be blind to it, or it was simply irrelevant in his quest to liberate him from the police station. Given this collusion, the role that parents have in sanctioning delinquency, albeit unintentionally or unconsciously, is marked.

Punishment: the efficacy of physical intervention

Debates about the lack of deterrence or adequate punishments for criminals in our society dominate much of the popular press and public opinion. Measures for dealing with rising crime rates and increasing violence are often regarded as totally inappropriate, and a popular and common assumption enshrined in the 'law and order' lobby is the harder the punishment, the more effective the deterrent. As this research has clearly indicated, the relationship between crime and punishment is far more complex than the simplicity of these arguments suggest, and reveals that the relationship between attitudes and actual behaviour is often a contradictory one.

In principle, Del and his contemporaries would have much in common with the 'law and order' lobby. They, like many more 'respectable' citizens argued that there was nothing to discourage children from crime nowadays, and felt that it was important for them to be 'frightened out' of it at an early age. Barry put his argument succinctly: 'They've got to be fuckin' downright ignorant with 'em.' As Del, Jimmy, and Barry had all been involved in crime and were recipients of some form of custodial sentences, their espousal of the importance of 'hard' methods might, at a superficial level, be used to support the 'law and order' viewpoint. However, such an approach would miss the crucial importance of their statements.

As I have illustrated throughout, the discrepancy between attitudes and actual behaviour was often significant. Yet Del, Jimmy, and Barry were rarely aware of the contradictions in their statements, as personal biographies could be acceptably excluded in the expression of general abstract opinions. Therefore the efficacy of the 'old', 'hard' methods could be upheld, despite their failure in reforming any of the men personally. Barry, for example, said:

> People say 'you're old fashioned', but the old-fashioned methods worked, they proved that, we aint got the crime rate in '68 that we got now. They've got nothink to discourage them at all. If he come up to me and said 'Dad, I've been nicked, looks like I'm gonna get three months DC'. I'd say 'All right boy, then do it', knowing full well he'd laugh, cos he gets so much about how easy it is and what to do there. Do you know there was a point in the paper, put on the same principle as when we were 16 or 17, everythink done on double time and I think somebody's trying to shut it down, or change the system right, but they had 95 per cent proof that them people have not gone back to crime – 95 per cent.

As I have illustrated, such arguments are more problematic than Barry suggests, and the distinction is often reduced to whether or not such incarceration enables people to learn how not to get caught again, rather than reforming them. For Barry this difference is inconsequential, as the extract indicates below. In terms of this discussion on the efficacy of punishment it is essential. I asked him:

JF: Have they gone back to crime, but just haven't been caught?

Barry: They haven't gone back to crime. All right they haven't got caught, put it any way you like.

JF: But there's a difference, isn't there?

Barry: In my DC, yer done yer bird, but you learn. You think right, I've either got to be twice as clever or you don't do it no more.

As the previous chapters have described at length, Barry, Del, and many of their friends, having learned the rudimentary rules of the game, learned how 'to be twice as clever' and not to get caught. The sentence itself, although hard, had little value or deterrent effect, as there was essentially nothing wrong with crime from their perspective. This is not to deny that in *some* cases detention can reduce the likelihood of re-offending, merely that it did not appear to be the case for Del, Barry, or Jimmy. Recidivism rates indicate, however, that this may be true for many more, as McDonald (1976: 15) realistically commented: 'there is now a whole literature showing that rehabilitation programmes do not rehabilitate and prevention programmes do not prevent.'

Accusations of soft and ineffectual methods for today's juvenile offenders did not emanate entirely from the 'good old days' philosophy, as considerable changes have occurred in juvenile justice policies over the twenty-year period with a shift away from custodial sentences (Ditchfield 1976). Yet, as West argues:

Despite all the rhetoric about soft treatment for juvenile offenders, the number of juveniles incarcerated in Prison Department establishments (borstals and detention centres) in England has increased dramatically in recent years.

(West 1982: 140)

The issue which dominated many of the discussions on punishment was hanging and the need for its reinstatement. This was perceived to be the only successful deterrent for serious offenders. Barry, for example, argued:

If you tell somebody they're gonna hang, if they kill somebody, they're not gonna do it and they think about it when they go in for armed robbery. They think, well if I shoot him, I could be up for murder and hang for it. But [doing] 15 years is nothink.

While Carol said:

I don't care what anybody says, before they abolished hanging, you never had all this, it was always safe to go out. I mean now, even in broad daylight you're not safe.

Despite their own experiences of injustice and outrage at being wrongly accused, there was little concern for those innocent people who might be hanged. Their attitude was that it was better to hang fifteen innocent people than let the guilty ones live. Hanging would not in fact alter behaviour because, as I have emphasised throughout, there was little relationship between crime and punishment in the mind of the offender at the time the act was committed. It was only after the event that such logic became apparent.

Considering solutions

People will change given the circumstances, given the chance.
People from our type of upbringing don't always get the chance.
(Jimmy)

This research began with the expectation that there would be little relationship between juvenile and adult crime, and that the experiences of two different generations of youths, divided by twenty years of significant social and economic change, would not be similar. Clearly the findings do not support this view and some of the reasons why continuity was more apparent than change have been described.

Although participant observation is not a methodology from which generalisations can readily be made, and in essence the findings presented here are relevant only to the small group of youths and adults with whom I was directly involved, the discussion in this concluding section addresses some of the issues I have raised in a more general manner and considers possible avenues for change.

Stott and Wilson (1977: 47) began an article in the British Journal of Criminology with the question:

Are criminals by-and-large typical members of an inner-city subculture who are unlucky in being caught, or do they form a special group even within their subculture?

Although the authors believed the latter statement to be most appropriate, I feel that the former is more appropriate. Crime is only one aspect of the inner city jigsaw; unemployment, bad housing, and low incomes are just some of the other factors which influence the lives of lower-class families in cities throughout Britain. Although individual and psychological theories may explain some forms of offending (particularly rape, child abuse, and some kinds of murder) 'crime' in its more common forms is far too widespread to be reduced to individual explanations alone, as criminal motivations are not unilinear, but differ according to the nature of the crime and the context of the offending behaviour.

Most debates about the causes of crime from varying theoretical and political perspectives usually begin by asking *why* people, especially working-class males, and juveniles in particular, become involved in crime. In terms of Del and those in the Grafton Arms, the question 'Why?' elicits the automatic response that there is 'nothing wrong' in it. This does not mean that they did not recognise the difference between right and wrong, or had no morality. They simply operated according to differing codes and standards, where 'doin' business' was seen as 'normal' and was not regarded as real 'crime' at all. Well-established techniques of neutralization defended and rationalized this position and allowed their abstract awareness that stealing was wrong to remain intact (especially as their behaviour could be compared with '*real*' criminals). Attitudes towards, and involvement in, certain kinds of crime were strongly influenced by cultural factors where crime was part of a highly rational process which offered semi-legitimate and illegitimate avenues to goods they might not otherwise afford.

Attitudes towards those whose 'official' role it was to prevent crime were shaped, as we have seen, by experience. They included a recognition that although the police were 'bastards' who flaunted the rules more than they did themselves, some individual officers were 'all right'. They highlighted the abuse of the system as a tool to detract from their own offending rather than as a point of outrage at such practices, as the police did no more than they themselves would do if they occupied a similar position. But, and this is crucial, Del and his contemporaries, their offspring, and the teenagers in the younger generation were powerless to change their position in the hierarchy. Instead they had to manipulate their environment as best they could and exploit opportunities as they presented themselves. Crime was one of those opportunities which in some cases offered better rewards than their position in the legitimate social structure might have achieved.

Given that crime was in many ways an understandable and 'normal' environmental response, considering avenues for change is not an easy task. Nevertheless the replication of experience was facilitated by a number of factors, one of the most important being underachievement in education. The sociology of education is littered with examples of how the working classes consistently underachieve (cf Douglas 1964, Douglas *et al.* 1968). Differing language codes (Bernstein 1959), teacher expectations, cultural factors, and poor family background all play a role in this failure. Although schools should attempt to overcome disadvantage, they more often end up reinforcing it. To prevent this replication some form of positive intervention to assist deprived children is required, preferably at pre-school age. Children must be encouraged by a variety of more imaginative teaching techniques and individual attention to stay in school, as the relationship between truancy and delinquency is an important one (see Chapter 3). At secondary level curriculums should have greater practical application where the relationship between abstract learning and occupational skills is more apparent.

There is nothing new in arguments for pre-school intervention. The question is rather more concerned with the kind of intervention and in what ways this can successfully break the cycle. Evidence from projects established in Britain and the United States suggests that although pre-school programmes have short-term benefits their long-term impact is more questionable (cf Clarke 1980, Clinard 1978). It may be that inequality continues to mar the lives of deprived children during their education because they do not receive adequate parental support and are subjected (even in pre-school initiatives) to vastly conflicting environments at home and in school. There is a real need to involve the parents as much as the child for such schemes to succeed, because as we have seen many working-class parents feel that there is little they can do to assist their child's progress.

While improving educational opportunity and pre-school projects for future generations are important, parental supervision also has a crucial role to play in relation to crime in high delinquency areas, as Harriet Wilson's study of deprived families in Birmingham indicated:

The families who exercised chaperonage and who tend to adhere to traditional standards of strictness ... share the belief that the deprived neighbourhood and its inhabitants are bad and that their children need protection against this badness.... These parents were driven into applying child rearing measures which, under normal conditions in a friendly and known neighbourhood, they would not be likely to apply. They kept their children indoors or under close supervision in the backyard; they accompanied them to and from school; they forbade them to play with undesirable youngsters in the streets. If the boys played out their mothers went to find them.

(Wilson and Herbert 1978: 176)

All these factors, as we have seen, were notably absent in descriptions of both the youths and men in this study. Girls had curfew restrictions and greater supervision throughout their formative years and perhaps this explains their relative absence from criminal involvement. Wilson found further confirmation for her arguments in a later study which she conducted, but also highlighted the importance of a non-judgemental approach where lack of parental supervision was not the 'fault' of individual parents, but the result of other social problems such families faced.

the essential point of our findings is the very close association of lax parenting with severe social handicap. Lax parenting methods are often the result of chronic stress, situations arising from frequent or prolonged spells of unemployment, physical or mental disabilities among members of the family, and an often permanent condition of poverty.... If these factors are ignored, and parental laxness is seen instead as an 'attitude' which by education or by punitive measures can be shifted, then our findings are being misrepresented. It is the position of the most disadvantaged groups in society and not the individual, which needs improvement in the first place.

(Wilson 1980: 223–4)

Recognising some of the difficulties which deprived families experience bringing up young children, a voluntary 'Home Start' scheme designed to provide practical help in the home before children are at risk (see Owen 1987) has been established in many parts of the country. It is perhaps by the use of such schemes which encourage and assist, rather than criticise and berate, poor families that we might see changes in cycles of offending in future generations.

Just as social factors offer better explanations for involvement in many forms of crime, taking the individual as the focus for possible change is not a very profitable way forward. Perhaps we must accept that, for certain people, crime is an activity in which they are frequently or infrequently involved and will continue to be so, and need to consider how we might prevent crime and make it less easy, rather than trying to reform them – because prevention is far easier than cure. As crime is undoubtedly related to opportunity (see Mayhew *et al.* 1976, Clarke 1980) 'situational' crime prevention provides a limited, but practical approach to dealing with some forms of crime (see Clarke and Mayhew 1980).

Critics of situational crime control rightly point out that crime prevention measures alone will not alleviate many of the structural problems faced by those in the inner cities who are involved in crime, and that we need to understand why people behave as they do. However, some schemes which have brought about a reduction in crime have had wider effects. Initiatives like the Priority Estates Projects (PEP) (Power 1987, 1989) consult and involve residents on poor inner city estates in building improvements and the implementation of crime prevention measures, such as better doors, lighting, and entry phone systems. These projects have, due to resident participation, brought about a reduction in crime, improved tenants' perceptions of their estates, and created a degree of self-policing and pride in the community, which ostracises those who attempt to damage or destroy what tenants have worked for. Although this has influenced levels of vandalism and criminal damage, which was a major pursuit of the youths in this study, it is far less likely to have any impact on the activities of the adult group, as these were sanctioned and widely utilised by the community.

It is also debatable whether crime prevention measures actually prevent or simply displace crime. In the case of the youths in this study, they stopped stealing from large well-equipped record stores because of their security measures and moved to smaller and less risky ones.

There will always be a certain level of crime committed not only by those in the lower strata of society but also by people who hold positions of trust and authority, although these may take a different form. It is too easy to regard the archetypal mugger or burglar as a menace to society and see crime as a working-class activity, related to poor social and economic conditions in inner city areas. While there are undoubtedly important and substantial relationships between certain types of crime and class, this is not by any means the entire picture. We must recognise that different crimes occur within differing contexts and are subject to varying kinds of intervention. In this respect, Del and his contemporaries were undoubtedly right when they argued 'there is one law for the rich and another for the poor.'

Conclusion

This book has described a small number of people in one area of South East London, people who were involved in activities which were often not regarded as crime at all. It indicates that there is more continuity in experience and attitudes between generations than has previously been suggested and reveals the strength and persistence of working-class values and attitudes. Within a specific cultural milieu, certain kinds of crimes were regarded as quite acceptable as 'everyone was at it'. Such practices had firm historical roots, passed from one generation to the next, and remained despite significant social and economic change. Involvement in the semi-legitimate or illegitimate sphere provided status and opportunity for the pursuit of 'easy money', where a differing set of standards and values (also deeply embedded) neutralised the 'wrongness' of such behaviour.

Unlike the literature, which draws firm distinctions between juvenile and adult crime, the former was an 'informal' apprenticeship and preparation for the latter. The juvenile years involved learning the basic rules of the community and how to 'play the game' in the highly visible public sphere. This resulted in attention from law-enforcement agencies which influenced the formation of attitudes, allowed the juvenile to learn the rudimentary rules of interaction with the police and how to minimise likely detection, arrest, and conviction. These experiences, in addition to the new opportunities which adult status afforded in terms of employment and the utilisation of the extended family network, brought about a transition from the public to the private sphere of crimes. At adulthood therefore, there was no commitment to give up crime or any significant shift in attitude from lawless to law abiding. These were not criminal 'careers', just ordinary people whose everyday world took for granted certain kinds of crime.

The social world I have described here no longer exists: research is always retrospective by the time of writing. In 1988, Del and Chris are separated, as are Barry and Sal. Jane and Tony are married with a child (born in 1986) and the Main Event and his friends have 'formally' left school. The Grafton is no longer a 'local', as the tenancy, which became vacant when Arthur and Vera moved to Kent, was taken by a black landlord. Such changes, although crucial in terms of setting and relationships, remain superficial compared with the importance of generational continuity. I doubt this will be true for the contemporary teenagers twenty years hence. Despite the appearance of a 'time warp', changes were taking place in the area, the most notable being migration, which in time will weaken extended family patterns and allegiance to 'tradition'. For the moment, however, the existence of kinship networks in a community with well-established forms of informal economic activities maintained semi-legitimate and illegitimate avenues to status, autonomy and control, and although unintentionally, reproduced attitudes and experience in subsequent generations. Crime was just taken for granted as another aspect of life where attitudes towards it, and those whose job it was to prevent it, had barely changed at all.

Notes

1 It was not that clothing and keeping 'in the pose' was an unimportant aspect of youth (Hebdige 1979). All the youths placed particular emphasis on their dress and spent a great deal of money on clothes but these were not fundamental points of differentiation from the parent generation.

2 Del, for example, was forced to move from his yard as a result of council policies. He argued that it was becoming difficult to find sites for yards because they were regarded as 'dirty, eye sores' and did not comply with council regulations on the environment.

3 Del described a similar incident which involved an interview with the P&O shipping company where he had applied to be a steward. 'They asked me to spell "funnel" and I spelt it with one "n". I got rejected, mainly because I told them that I didn't know anybody who'd be asking for a "funnel sandwich", I reckon they should have had OXO! They didn't think I had the right attitude towards the job. What sort of attitude are you supposed to have to put a plate down in front of someone?'

4 Shover (1985: 83) argues that 'the ageing process of ordinary property offenders includes a redefinition of their youthful criminal identity as self-defeating, foolish or "stupid".' As the children's own parents had reached the beginnings of such an evaluation process, this may have contributed to their portrayal of delinquency as 'silly'.

Appendix: some considerations on methodology

Although all research methods have advantages and disadvantages, participant observation is probably the most controversial (cf McCall and Simmons 1969). This appendix describes the history of the research and some of the issues and dilemmas which emerged during the fieldwork.

One of the questions which is always asked of participant observers is *how* they got in. Like other research of this kind, access for me came about as a result of a chance meeting with Chris. She offered to introduce me to some of her friends who had offended in their youth and socialised in the Grafton Arms, but suggested that the nature of my research should remain covert. I was therefore introduced as Janet, who was a student, and wanted to join the ladies' darts team. Here began the first of many learning experiences (since I had never played darts!) and the first of several ethical dilemmas. I began by visiting the Grafton on ladies' darts night and within a short time was a regular in the pub most evenings of the week. The darts provided me with an excellent opportunity to mix with the men and gave me a 'legitimate' reason for being there. As I was keen to learn they all took a great deal of time and patience (with my appalling subtraction!) helping me.

I never made any attempt to speak or dress differently, and my accent presented few problems. One person described me as 'working class with a nice accent!', while others explained it as a product of my roots. George, for example, defended me when one of her 'mates' commented, 'Your friend's a bit posh, ain't she?' George replied, 'Janet comes from Bournemouth and they all speak like that down there!'

Being small, young, and female was a decided advantage in negotiating most aspects of the field. People always responded to me primarily as a woman and secondarily as a student who was doing a 'project' or writing a book – a task which was not viewed very seriously. Hammersley and Atkinson (1983: 84) argue that while it is not possible to have a 'position of genderless neutrality' (cf Roberts 1981), 'cultural stereotypes of females can work to their advantage' and for me this proved to be very much the case. With the exception of the youth, I became something of a 'mascot' (Easterday *et al.* 1982), referred to as 'little Janet' or that 'nice young lady', and people often teased and joked with me about my size.

Although Chris's advice and assistance were invaluable in terms of the 'normality' of the research setting and my acceptance as 'one of the girls', they created particular difficulties later in the research as I was concerned that my cover might be 'blown' (cf Hammersley and Atkinson 1983: 94). In practice such matters are often more simple than a researcher's anxiety allows for. As Gans (1962: 345) noted: 'Most people are too busy living to take much notice of a participant-observer once he [she!] has proven to them that he means no harm.'

After six months of covert observation, I mentioned to Chris that I would like to interview some of the couples in the Grafton and by the time I arrived in the pub that evening she had spoken to most of them: they all expressed willingness to assist me with my 'project'! All of the main couples in the public bar, apart from Vera and Arthur, and Billy, who moved out of the area during the research, were interviewed in their homes. Most were interviewed on three separate occasions over a number of weeks. The semi-structured interviews focused first on childhood and teenage years, the second on the period between leaving school and their mid-20s and a third on present-day life and more general attitudes. All these interviews were tape recorded.

The youth in both age groups were drawn from a snowball sample of Del's and Chris's two children. Although this allowed me to trace the direct relationship between father and son, it was far from ideal, as my close contact with their parents caused natural suspicion and mistrust among the youths. Both my expectations and the mechanics of the youth research were rather naive at the outset. Without a doubt this was the most physically strenuous and weakest part of the fieldwork. It is difficult to comprehend the distance that exists between adults and youths in their manner of behaving. Goffman (1955) notes the importance of maintaining a 'personal front' and this was pushed to its limit in relation to the youths. Their unstructured existence was a constant source of difficulty for me, from purely practical problems of organising the research, to the disquiet and inner apprehension I experienced as a result of their activities. I not only observed their behaviour and noted their reasons and rationalisations, but also considered the result of their actions. When they threw bin liners filled with rubbish and glass from a third-floor balcony without a thought, I considered the dangers; when they victimised elderly tenants I inwardly cringed. As these things occurred largely below the surface and the youths were unaware of them, they did not seriously impair my rapport with the boys. From their perspective, I was 'not bad for a woman', as I could run and keep up with them and did not appear to be influenced by their behaviour or chastise them for it.

A total of five months was spent in observation and interviews with both groups of teenagers. As it was rare for them to spend evenings at home, interviews and group discussions took place in my council flat.

Although the boys in the younger group were initially quite reticent in my presence and very aware of my femininity, once I had been accepted I became something of a token man. This proved to be a considerable barrier in my relationship with the girls, who 'hung out' on the street corner separately. They had no point of contact with me, as I was unlike any of the women they knew. One of the younger girls asked me on one occasion if I was a 'real' woman (cf Horowitz 1983) and regarded me as 'abnormal' for choosing to spend my time with the boys, rather than 'looking after a man and having babies'. While the boys enjoyed the novelty of taking part in the research (which I described as writing a book about the area) the girls refused to be interviewed, despite several attempts by myself and the boys to encourage them to do so.

Ethical dilemmas are inevitable in participant observation and are largely resolved in the field. Polsky deals succinctly with my stance on illegal activities:

> If one is to effectively study adult criminals in their natural setting, he must make the moral decision that in some ways he will break the law himself. He need not be a 'participant' observer and commit the criminal acts under study, yet he has to witness such acts or be taken into confidence about them and not blow the whistle.
>
> (Polsky, 1971: 138)

This latter position posed few problems for me: to 'blow the whistle' would have negated the purpose of the research and would certainly not have been in my personal interest. However, I must also state that I never received stolen goods and was largely exempted from any necessity to do so as the network was almost entirely male.

Ethical questions were often more direct in the case of the younger group of youths. On one occasion they invited me to join them breaking into a cinema to see a film. It was yet one more example of researcher anxiety when I considered possible ways to deal with their invitation, without being regarded as a 'chicken' and altering the group's perception of me. In the event it was not a problem. I told them that I would accompany them to the cinema but would pay to go in, since I might make a mistake and get everyone caught. While this produced an initial response that 'Janet was shit scared' (which indeed she was!) they rationalized it by arguing that as an adult, getting caught would have far greater repercussions for me, and that for this reason, my suggestion was a good one. Parker reports a similar attitude among the youths whom he observed. He argued:

> I would receive 'knock-off' and 'say nothing'. If necessary I would 'keep dixy' but I would not actually get my hands dirty. This stance was regarded as normal and surprised nobody; it coincided with the view of most adults in the neighbourhood. Further given my job, relative affluence and 'middle-classness', it was also regarded as an expedient stance. I had things to lose by getting caught.
>
> (Parker 1974: 218–19)

My femininity again excluded me from any need to receive and the boys trusted that I would not go to the police.

The second part of the youth study arose from a snowball sample of Chris's and Del's elder son, Tony. As with the younger group, it took a great deal of time to establish links, and it was finally through Jane, a young woman I had met in the Grafton Arms, that I gained access. I was introduced as someone who was writing a book about the area, which, after initial caution, was enthusiastically endorsed as a worthwhile task because they felt it was important that people outside, especially those in universities who were 'out of touch', knew what the area and living there was like.

During this stage of the fieldwork, Pete's parents were abroad, and as a result the five weeks of intensive observation wih this group was largely unrepresentative of their normal behaviour. I made sure that I asked each of them just how representative my observations had been in relation to their usual behaviour. They argued that they spent more time driving around in their cars, having races, sniffing Tippex, and 'doing nothing', but that the manner they related to each other and their descriptions of their activities were similar.

It had not been my original intention at the outset of the research to observe the police in the area. However, as the work progressed, I felt that it would be useful to spend a short time with them, observing their behaviour and gathering information about their attitudes towards the area. I spent eight weeks at two local police stations, accompanying officers patrolling on foot and in vehicles. I also interviewed fifteen police officers (two chief inspectors, two sergeants, two WPCs, and nine PCs, including two probationers) most of whom had considerable knowledge of the area and had policed the ground for many years.

I had been extremely fortunate not to experience any direct confrontation with the police during other stages of the fieldwork, so I was neither known by them, nor associated with any particular group. Having gained the confidence of both the adults and youths, I told them I was going to spend a few weeks with the 'Old Bill', which they readily accepted, some saying it was a good idea so I could see 'what they were really like'. It was agreed that if I encountered any of them whilst accompanying an officer they would not acknowledge me. On two occasions, Del and Jimmy could not resist the urge of shouting from their vehicles when I was walking with officers! However, overt contact where police actually dealt with individuals I knew occurred only on two or three occasions, the most serious during a CID investigation.

It is always important in participant observation to maintain some distance from the social world one is observing. Although I grew to like some of the people in the study and got to know many of their personal lives in a reasonably detailed way (which produced a sense of guilt when the work was completed) I still regarded their activities as 'wrong' just as they regarded them as quite acceptable. It is this distance which is crucial for the participant observer, as Hammersley and Atkinson (1983: 102) note: 'There must always remain some part held back, some social and intellectual "distance". For it is in the "space" created by this distance that the analytic work of the ethnographer gets done.'

Standing back and taking stock

Unlike other methods in ethnography, theory emerges from practice. Often areas which acquire crucial importance in the later stages of research seem to have no obvious significance at the outset.

Consequently there are areas of my research, particularly with regard to opportunity structures, which I have less information about than I would like, and had they been clearer to me during the fieldwork I would have looked into them in more detail.

There is also the question of validity. Inevitably the numbers who participated in this study were small and, as I have indicated, some groups were easier to study than others. Validation, however, was possible to a certain degree, as the social networks of the different generations were quite restricted, while my observations with the police confirmed my belief that the subjects were fairly typical. Obviously this is subject to my own interpretation and the evidence is only impressionistic. Ianni deals with the issue of validity by posing two questions. He wrote:

> My training and subsequent field experience have convinced me that direct observation of human action is better than the collection of verbal statements about that action if one would understand how a social system functions. I place great reliance on observing and recording only what I have seen, and so the question of validity is really two questions: Did I see what I thought I was seeing? Did the actors perform naturally, or were they attempting to mask their behaviour?

(Ianni and Reuss-Ianni 1972: 182)

In response to these questions, I believe I saw many of the processes which operated, but certainly not all of them; like every researcher I have been selective in the presentation of my material, and may have missed aspects which others would have regarded as important. In terms of behaviour, it was probably most 'normal' in the pub, as my purpose for being there was covert, but was not a serious problem with any of the groups once they became accustomed to my presence.

I would, however, like to add a third assessment to Ianni's on the question of validity, which does not involve the use of participant observation but concerns research strategies in general. For me, the quest of all forms of sociology is to understand the social world, using whatever methodologies a researcher believes can elicit data. In terms of attitudes and their relation to behaviour the mode of enquiry I employed allowed me to place attitudes within a behavioural and cultural context. I wholeheartedly agree with Becker that we ought to see [deviant behaviour] simply as a kind of behaviour some disappprove of and others value, studying the processes by which either or both perspectives are built up and maintained. Perhaps the best surety against either extreme is close contact with the people we study.

(Becker 1963: 176)

References

Adler, F. (1975) *Sisters in Crime*, New York: McGraw Hill.

Bartles-Smith, D. and Gerrard, D. (1976) *Urban Ghetto*, London: Guildford.

Becker, H.S. (1963) *Outsiders: Studies in the Sociology of Deviance*, London: The Free Press.

Becker, H.S. (1970) *Sociological Work: Method and Substance*, Chicago: Aldine.

Bennett, T. (1979) 'The Social Distribution of Criminal Labels: Police "Proaction" or "Reaction?"', *British Journal of Criminology* Vol 19, No 2, April 1979, pp 134– 45.

Benyon, J. (ed.) 1984) *Scarman and After: Essays Reflecting on Lord Scarman's Report, the Riots and Their Aftermath*, Oxford: Pergamon Press.

Bernstein, B. (1959) 'A Public Language: Some Sociological Implications of a Linguistic Form', *British Journal of Sociology* Vol 10, pp 311–26.

Black, J. (1930) 'A Burglar Looks at Laws and Codes', *Harpers Magazine* Vol CLX, No 957, February, p 306.

Blagg, H. (1985) 'Reparation and Justice for Juveniles: The Corby Experience', *British Journal of Criminology* Vol 25, No 7, pp 267–79.

Booth, C. (1889-91) *Life and Labour of the People of London*, three volumes, London: Williams & Norgate.

Bott, E. (1957) *Family and Social Network: Roles, Norms, and External Relationships in Ordinary Urban Families*, London: Tavistock.

Bottoms, A. and McClintock, F. (1973) *Criminals Coming of Age: A Study of Institutional Adaption in the Treatment of Adolescent Offenders*, London: Heinemann.

Box, S. and Hale, C. (1983) 'Liberation and Female Criminality in England and Wales', *British Journal of Criminology* Vol 23, No 1, January 1983, pp 35–49.

Boyle, J. (1977) *A Sense of Freedom*, London: Pan.

Brake, M. (1973) 'Cultural Revolution or Alternative Delinquency - An Examination of Deviant Youth as a Social Problem', in Bailey, R. and

Young, J. (eds) *Contemporary Social Problems in Britain*, Farnborough: Saxon House.

Brake, M. (1980) *The Sociology of Youth Culture and Youth Subcultures: Sex and Drugs and Rock 'n' Roll?*, London: Routledge & Kegan Paul.

Brake, M. (1985) *Comparative Youth Culture: The Sociology of Youth Cultures and Youth Subcultures in America, Britain and Canada*, London: Routledge & Kegan Paul.

Brown, B. and Altman, I. (1981) 'Territoriality and Residential Crime: A Conceptual Framework', in Brantingham, P. and Brantingham, P. (eds) *Environmental Criminology*, Beverly Hills, Calif.: Sage.

Brown, W.K. (1977) 'Black Women's Gangs in Philadelphia', *International Journal of Offender Therapy and Comparative Criminology* Vol 21, No 3, pp 221–8.

Burney, E. (1976) *Housing on Trial: A Study of Immigrants and Local Government*, Institute of Racial Relations, London: Oxford University Press.

Cameron, M.O. (1964) *The Booster and The Snitch: Department Store Shoplifting*, New York: The Free Press.

Campbell, A. (1981) *Girl Delinquents*, Oxford: Blackwell.

Campbell, A. (1984a) *The Girls in the Gang: A Report from New York City*, Oxford: Blackwell.

Campbell, A. (1984b) 'The Girls in the Gang', *New Society* 20 Sept, pp 308–311.

Carlen, P. (1976) *Magistrates' Justice*, London: Martin Robertson.

Cashmore, E. (1984) *No Future: Youth and Society*, London: Heinemann.

Cavan, S. (1966) *Liquor License: An Ethnography of Bar Behaviour*, Chicago: Aldine.

Chappell, D. and Walsh, M. (1974) 'Operational Parameters in the Stolen Property System', *Journal of Criminal Justice* Vol 2, pp 113–29.

Chesney, K. (1970) *The Victorian Underworld*, London: Temple Smith.

Clarke, P. and Hedges, B. (1976) *Living in Southwark*, London: Social and Community Planning Research.

Clarke, R.V.G. (1980) 'Situational Crime Prevention: Theory and Practice', *British Journal of Criminology* Vol 20, No 2, April 1980, pp 136–47.

Clarke, R.V.G. (1984) 'Opportunity-based Crime Rates: The Difficulties of Further Refinement', *British Journal of Criminology* Vol 24, No 1, January 1984, pp 74–83.

Clarke, R.V.G. and Mayhew, P. (eds) (1980) *Designing Out Crime*, London: HMSO.

Clinard, M. (1978) *Cities with Little Crime: The Case of Switzerland*, Cambridge: Cambridge University Press.

Cloward, R.A. and Ohlin, L.E. (1960) *Delinquency and Opportunity: A Theory of Delinquent Gangs*, London: The Free Press.

Coates, K. and Silburn, R. (1970) *Poverty: The Forgotten Englishman,* Harmondsworth: Penguin.

Cohen, A.K. (1955) *Delinquent Boys, The Culture of the Gang,* Glencoe Ill: The Free Press.

Cohen, P. (1972) *Working Class Youth Cultures in East London,* Working Papers in Cultural Studies 2, Birmingham University.

Coleman, A. (1985) *Utopia On Trial: Vision and Reality in Planned Housing,* London Hilary Shipman.

Colquhoun, P. (1800) *A Treatise on the Commerce and the Police of the River Thames,* London: printed for Joseph Mawman.

CRE (Commission for Racial Equality) (1984) *Race and Council Housing in Hackney - Report of a Formal Investigation,* London: Commission for Racial Equality.

Corrigan, P. (1979) *Schooling the Smash Street Kids,* London: Macmillan

Cressey, D.R. (1953) *Other People's Money: A Study in the Social Psychology of Embezzlement,* Glencoe, Ill: The Free Press.

Dalton, M (1959) *Men Who Manage: Fusions of Feeling and Theory in Administration,* New York: Wiley.

Deakin, N. and Ungerson, C. (1973) 'Beyond the Ghetto: The Illusion of Choice', in Donnison, D. and Eversley, D. (eds) *London: Urban Patterns, Problems and Policies,* a study sponsored by the Centre for Environmental Studies, London: Heinemann.

Dennis, H., Henriques, F. and Slaughter, C. (1956) *Coal is Our Life: An Analysis of a Yorkshire Mining Community,* London: Eyre & Spottiswoode.

Ditchfield, J. (1976) *Police Cautioning in England and Wales,* Home Office Research Unit, Study No 37 London: HMSO

Ditton, J. (1976) '"The Fiddler": A Sociological Analysis of Forms of Blue Collar Employee Theft among Bread Salesmen', Ph.D. Thesis, University of Durham. Quoted in Henry, S. (1978).

Ditton, J. (1977) *Part Time Crime: An Ethnography of Fiddling and Pilferage,* London: Macmillan.

Douglas, J.W.B. (1964) *The Home and the School: A Study of Ability and Attainment in the Primary School,* London: MacGibbon & Kee.

Douglas, J.W.B., Ross, J.M., and Simpson, H.R. (1968) *All Our Futures: A Longitudinal Study of Secondary Education,* London: Peter Davies.

Downes, D. (1966) *The Delinquent Solution: A Study in Subcultural Theory,* London: Routledge & Kegan Paul.

Durkheim, E. (1964) *The Rules of Sociological Method,* New York: The Free Press.

Easterday, L., Papademas, D., Schorr, L. and Valentine, C. (1982) 'The Makings of a Female Researcher: Role Problems in Fieldwork', in Burgess, R. G. (ed.) *Field Research: A Sourcebook and Field Manual,* London: Allen & Unwin.

Farrington, D., Gallagher, L., Morey, L, St Ledger, R.J. and West, D.J. (1986) 'Unemployment, School Leaving and Crime', *British Journal of Criminology* Vol 26, No 4, October, pp 335–56.

Ferguson, T. (1952) *The Young Delinquent in his Social Setting: A Glasgow Study*, London: published for the Nuffield Foundation by Oxford University Press.

Fernando, E. and Hedges, B. (1976) *Moving Out of Southwark*, London: Social and Community Planning Research, Centre for Sample Surveys.

Firth, R. and Djamour, J. (1956) 'Kinship in South Borough', in Firth, R. (ed.) *Two Studies of Kinship in London*, London School of Economics, Monographs on Social Anthropology, No 15, London: The Athlone Press.

Foster, J.A. (1987) 'Culture and Community: Attitudes in Two Generations to Crime and Law Enforcement in South East London' unpublished Ph.D. Thesis, University of London.

Foster, J.A. (1988) 'Crime and Community: An Ethnographic Evaluation of Two London Housing Estates', unpublished report for Home Office, London: Research and Planning Unit.

Foster, J.A. (1989) 'Two Stations: An Ethnographic Study of Policing in the Inner City', in Downes, D. (ed.) *Crime and the City: Essays in Honour of John Mays*, London: Macmillan.

Fyvel, T.R. (1963) *The Insecure Offenders, Rebellious Youth in the Welfare State*, Harmondsworth: Penguin.

Gans, H. (1962) *The Urban Villagers: Group and Class in the Life of Italian Americans*, New York: The Free Press.

Gill, O. (1977) *Luke Street: Housing Policy, Conflict and the Creation of the Delinquency Area*, London: Macmillan Press.

Gittus, E. (1969) 'Sociological Aspects of Urban Decay', in Medhurst, F. and Parry Lewis, J. (eds) *Urban Decay, An Analysis and a Policy*, London: Macmillan.

Glass, R. (1960) *Newcomers: The West Indians in London*, London: Centre for Urban Studies.

Glueck, S. and Glueck, E. (1930) *500 Criminals*, New York: Knopf.

Glueck, S. and Glueck, E. (1940) *Juvenile Delinquents Grown Up*, New York: Commonwealth Fund.

Glueck, S. and Glueck, E. (1943) *Criminal Careers in Retrospect*, New York: Commonwealth Fund

Glueck, S. and Glueck, E. (1950) *Unravelling Juvenile Delinquency*, Commonwealth Fund: Oxford University Press

Glueck, S. and Glueck, E. (1968) *Delinquents and Non-Delinquents in Perspective*, Cambridge, Mass: Harvard University Press.

Glueck, S. and Glueck, E. (1974) *Of Delinquency and Crime: A Panorama of Years of Search and Research*, Springfield, Ill: Charles C. Thomas.

Goffman, E. (1955) 'On Face-Work: An Analysis of Ritual Elements in Social Interaction', *Psychiatry* Vol 18, No 3, pp 213–31.

Goldthorpe, J.H., Lockwood, D., Bechhofer, F., and Platt, J. (1969) *The Affluent Worker in the Class Structure*, three volumes, London: Cambridge University Press.

Gorham, M. and Dunnett, H. (1950) *Inside the Pub*, London: Architectural Press.

Greater London Council (1974/5/6) 'Research Report 21: Colour and the Allocation of Council Housing: The Report of the GLC Lettings Survey', London: GLC.

Griffin, C. (1982) 'Cultures of Femininity: Romance Revisited', CCCS Stencilled Occasional Paper, Women Series, No 69.

Griffin, C. (1984) 'Young Women and Work: The Transition from School to Labour Market for Young Working Class Girls', CCCS, University of Birmingham, No 76.

Griffin, C. (1985) *Typical Girls?: Young Women from School to the Job Market*, London: Routledge & Kegan Paul.

Hall, J. (1935) *Theft, Law and Society*, Boston, Mass: Little Brown.

Hall, S. and Jefferson, T. (eds) (1976) *Resistance Through Rituals*, London: Hutchinson.

Hammersley, M. and Atkinson, P. (1983) *Ethnography: Principles in Practice*, London: Tavistock.

Hamnett, C. (1986) 'Who Gets to Own?, *New Society* 25 July 1986, pp 18–19.

Hargreaves, D. (1967) *Social Relations in a Secondary School*, London: Routledge and Kegan Paul.

Harrison, T. (ed.) (1943) 'Mass Observation' The Pub and the People: A Worktown Study, London: Gollancz.

Haslam, S. (undated) *Interviewing Young People about Juvenile Crime*, Report for NACRO Juvenile Crime Unit.

Hebdige, D. (1977) *Subcultural Conflict and Criminal Performance in Fulham*, Occasional paper, Sub and Popular Culture Series, No 25, Centre for Contemporary Cultural Studies, Birmingham.

Hebdige, D. (1979) *Subculture: The Meaning of Style*, London: Methuen.

Heidensohn, F. (1985) *Women and Crime*, Basingstoke: Macmillan.

Henry, S. (1978) *The Hidden Economy: The Context and Control of Borderline Crime*, London: Martin Robertson.

Hey, V. (1986) *Patriachy and Pub Culture*, London: Tavistock.

Hobbs, D. (1988) *Doing the Business: Entrepreneurship, the Working Class, and Detectives in East London*, Oxford: Clarendon Press.

Hoggart, R. (1957) *The Uses Of Literacy: Aspects of Working-Class Life, with Special References to Publications and Entertainment*, London: Chatto & Windus.

Horning, D.M. (1970) *Blue Collar Theft by Shop Staff: A Report of a Home Office Working Party on Internal Shop Security*, London: HMSO.

Horowitz, R. (1983) *Honor and the American Dream: Culture and Identity in a Chicago Community*, New Brunswick, NJ: Rutgers University Press.

Ianni, F.A.J. and Reuss-Ianni, E. (1972) *A Family Business*, London: Routledge & Kegan Paul.

Jowell, R. and Witherspoon, S. (eds) (1985) *British Social Attitudes: The 1985 Report*, Social and Community Planning Research, Aldershot, Hants: Gower.

Kerr, M. (1958) *The People of Ship Street*, London: Routledge & Kegan Paul.

Klein, J. (1965) *Samples from English Cultures*, London: Routledge & Kegan Paul.

Klockars, C. (1975) *The Professional Fence*, London: Tavistock.

Labov, W. (1972) 'The Transformation of Experience in Narrative Syntax' in W. Labov (ed.) *Language in the Inner City*, Philadelphia, Pa: Pennsylvania University Press.

Lambert, J., Paris, C. and Blackby, B. (1978) *Housing Policy and the State*, London: Macmillan.

Lees, S. (1986) *Losing Out: Sexuality and Adolescent Girls*, London: Hutchinson.

Levens, O.E. (1964) 'One Hundred and One White Collar Criminals', *New Society* 26 March pp 6–8.

Liebow, E. (1967) *Tally's Corner: A Study of Negro Street Corner Men*, Boston, Mass: Little, Brown.

Lipset, S.M. (1960) *Political Man*, London: Heinemann.

Lucas, N. (1969) *Britain's Gangland: Violence is their Way of Life*, London: Pan.

Luckenbill, D.F. and Best, J. (1981) 'Careers in Deviance and Respectability: The Analogy's Limitations', *Social Problems* Vol 29, No 2, pp 197–206.

McCall, G.J. and Simmons, J.L. (1969) (eds) *Issues in Participant Observation: A Text and Reader*, Reading, Mass: Addison-Wesley.

McDonald, L. (1976) *The Sociology Of Law and Order*, London.

McIntosh, M. (1978) 'Who Needs Prostitutes? The Ideology of Male Sexual Needs', in Smart, C. and Smart, B. (eds) *Women, Sexuality and Social Control*, London: Routledge & Kegan Paul.

Mack, J. (1964) 'Fulltime Miscreants, Delinquent Neighbourhoods and Criminal Networks', *British Journal of Sociology* Vol 15, pp 38–53.

McRobbie, A. (1978) 'Working Class Girls and the Culture of Feminity', in *Women's Study Group, CCCS, Women Take Issue*, Birmingham University, London: Hutchinson.

McRobbie, A. (1980) 'Settling Accounts with Subcultures: A Feminist Critique', *Screen Education*, Vol 34, pp 37–49.

McRobbie, A. (1982) 'The Politics of Feminist Research: Between Talk Text and Action', *Feminist Review* No 12, pp 46–57.

McRobbie, A. and Garber, J. (1976) 'Girls and Subcultures' in Hall, S. and Jefferson, T. (eds) *Resistance Through Rituals*, London: Hutchinson.

McVicar, J. (1974) *McVicar by Himself*, London: Hutchinson.

Mansfield, P. and Collard, J. (1988) *The Beginning of the Rest of your Life: A Portrait of Newly Wed Marriage*, London: Macmillan.

Mars, G. (1982) *Cheats at Work: An Anthropology of Workplace Crime*, London: Allen & Unwin.

Martin, J.P. (1962) *Offenders as Employees*, Vol XVI of the Cambridge Studies in Criminology, London: Macmillan.

Matza, D. (1964) *Delinquency and Drift*, London: John Wiley.

May, D. (1975) 'Truancy, School Absenteeism and Delinquency', *Scottish Educational Studies* 17, pp 97–107.

Mayer, M.O. (1980) *The Hard Core Delinquent*, Farnborough: Saxon House.

Mayhew, P., Clarke, R.V.G., Sturman, A. and Hough, J.M. (1976) *Crime as Opportunity*, HMSO.

Mays, J.B. (1954) *Growing Up in the City: A Study of Juvenile Delinquency in an Urban Neighbourhood*, Liverpool University Press.

Miller, W.B. (1958) 'Lower Class Culture as Generating Milieu of Gang Delinquency', *Journal of Social Issues* Vol 14, pp 5–19.

Mills, C. (1940) 'Situated Actions and Vocabularies of Motive', *American Sociological Review* Vol 5, pp 904–13.

Mogey, J. (1956) *Family and Neighbourhood: Two Studies in Oxford*, Oxford University Press.

Mungham, G. (1976) 'Youth in Pursuit of Itself', in Mungham, G. and Pearson, G. (eds) *Working Class Youth Culture*, London: Routledge & Kegan Paul.

Newman, O. (1972) *Defensible Space: Crime Prevention through Urban Design*, New York: Macmillan.

Nissel, M. (1982) 'Family and Social Change since the Second World War', in Rapoport, R.N. and Fogarty, M.P. (eds) *Families in Britain*, British Committee for Family Research, London: Routledge & Kegan Paul.

Nuttall, J. (1968) *Bomb Culture*, London: MacGibbon & Kee

Oliver, I.T. (1973) 'The Metropolitan Police Juvenile Bureau System', *Criminal Law Review* August, pp 449–506.

Oliver, I.T. (1978) *The Metropolitan Police Approach to the Prosecution of Juvenile Offenders*, London: Peel Press

OPCS (1981) *Census Results: Small Area Statistics*, London: HMSO.

Owen, K. (1987) 'Strength in Weakness', *New Society* 23 January, pp 24.

Parker, B.J. (1973) 'Some Sociological Implications of Slum Clearance Programmes', in Donnison, D. and Eversley, D., *London: Urban Patterns, Problems and Policies*, pp 248–73. A study sponsored by the Centre for Environmental Studies, London: Heinemann.

Parker, H.J. (1974) *View from the Boys: A Sociology of Down-Town Adolescents*, Newton Abbott: David & Charles.

Parker, H.J. (1976) 'Boys will be Men: Brief Adolescence in a Down Town Neighbourhood', in Mungham, G. and Pearson, G. (eds) *Working Class Youth Culture*, London: Routledge & Kegan Paul.

Parker, R. (1981) *Rough Justice*, London: Fontana.

Parker, T. (1967) *A Man of Good Abilities* London: Hutchinson.

Parker, T. and Allerton, R. (1962) *The Courage of his Convictions*, London: Hutchinson.

Patrick, J. (1973) *A Glasgow Gang Observed*, London: Eyre Methuen.

Pearson, G. (1983) *Hooligan: A History of Respectable Fears*, London: Macmillan.

Pearson, J. (1983) *The Profession of Violence: The Rise and Fall of the Kray Twins*, originally published 1972, London: Weidenfeld & Nicolson.

Piliavin, I.M. and Briar, S. (1964) 'Police Encounters with Juveniles'. *American Journal of Sociology* Vol 70, September, pp 206–14.

Polsky, N. (1971) *Hustlers, Beats, and Others*, Harmondsworth: Pelican.

Power, A. (1984) *Local Housing Management: A Priority Estates Project Survey*, London: Department of the Environment.

Power, A. (1987) *Property Before People: The Management of Twentieth Century Council Housing*, London: Allen & Unwin.

Power, A. (1989) 'Housing, Poverty and Crime', in Downes, D. (ed.) *Crime and the City: Essays in Tribute of John Mays*, London: Macmillan.

Read, P. P. (1984) *The Train Robbers: Their Story*, originally published 1978, London: W. H. Allen.

Rex, J. and Moore, R. (1967) *Race, Community and Conflict: A Study of Sparkbrook*, Oxford University Press, published for the Institute of Race Relations.

Roberts, H. (ed.) (1981) *Doing Feminine Research*, London: Routledge & Kegan Paul.

Rock, P. (1987) Personal conversation.

Roselius, T. and Benton, D. (1973) 'Marketing Theory and the Fencing of Stolen Goods', *Denver Law Journal* Vol 50, pp 177–205.

Scarman, Lord (1981) *The Brixton Disorders 10–12 April 1981: A Report of an Enquiry*, Cmnd 8427, London: HMSO.

Shacklady Smith, L. (1978) 'Sexist Assumptions and Female Delinquency: An Empirical Investigation', in Smart, C. and Smart, B. (eds) *Women, Sexuality and Social Control*, London: Routledge & Kegan Paul.

Sharpe, S. (1976) *Just Like a Girl: How Girls Learn to be Women*, Harmondsworth: Penguin.

Shaw, C. and McKay, H. (1942) *Juvenile Delinquency and Urban Areas*, Chicago: University of Chicago Press.

Shaw, J. (1978) 'School Attendance: Some Notes on a Further Feature of Sexual Division', paper given at conference on 'Patriarchy, Capitalism and Educational Policy' at the London Institute and Education, quoted in Griffen, C. (1985) *Typical Girls* London: Routledge & Kegan Paul.

Shover, N. (1985) *Aging Criminals*, Beverly Hills, Calif: Sage

Smith, R.B. and Stephans (1976) 'Drug Use and "Hustling" - A Study of their Relationships', *Criminology* Vol 14, pp 155–76.

Smith, S. (1986) 'The Wife's Sentence', *New Society* 21 November, pp 11–13.

South London Press Various editions.

Stacey, M. (1960) *Tradition and Change: A Study of Banbury*, London: Oxford University Press.

Stedman-Jones, G. (1971) *Outcast London: A Study in Relationships between Classes in Victorian Society*, Oxford: Oxford University Press.

Stott, D.H. and Wilson, D.M. (1977) 'The Adult Criminal as Juvenile: A Follow-up Study of Glasgow Juvenile Delinquents into Adulthood', *British Journal of Criminology* Vol 17, No 1, January 1977, pp 47–57.

Sutherland, E. (1949) 'White Collar Crime', New York: Holt, Rinehart & Winston.

Suttles, G.D. (1972) *The Social Construction of Communities*, Chicago: University of Chicago Press.

Sykes, G. and Matza, D. (1957) 'Techniques of Neutralization: A Theory of Delinquency', *American Sociological Review* Vol 22, No 6, pp 664–70.

Sykes, G. and Matza, D. (1961) 'Juvenile Delinquency and Subterranean Values', *American Sociological Review* Vol 26, pp 712–19.

Szasz, T. (1973) *The Second Sin*, London: Routledge & Kegan Paul.

Tannenbaum, F. (1938) *Crime and the Community*, New York: Columbia University Press.

Taylor, L. (1985) *In the Underworld*, originally published 1984, Oxford: Blackwell.

Tennett, T.G. (1971) 'School Non Attendance and Delinquency', *Educational Research* Vol 13, pp 185–90.

Townsend, P. (1957) *The Family Life of Old People: An Inquiry in East London*, London: Routledge & Kegan Paul.

Townsend, P. (1979) *Poverty in the United Kingdom: A Survey of Household Resources and Standards of Living*, Harmondsworth: Penguin.

Ungerson, C. (1971) 'Moving Home: A Study of the Redevelopment Process in two London Boroughs', *Occasional Papers on Social Administration 44*, London: Bell.

Wallman, S. (1982) *Living in South London: Perspectives on Battersea 1871–1981*, Aldershot: published for the LSE by Gower.

Welsh, S. (1981) 'The Manufacture of Excitement in Police-Juvenile Encounters', *British Journal of Criminology* Vol 21, No 3, July 1981, pp 257–67.

West, D.J. (1967) *The Young Offender*, London: Duckworth.

West, D.J. (1969) *Present Conduct and Future Delinquency: First Report of the Cambridge Study in Delinquent Development* London: Heinemann.

West, D.J. (1982) *Delinquency: Its Roots, Careers and Prospects*, London: Heinemann.

West, D.J. and Farrington, D. P. (1973) *Who Becomes Delinquent? Second Report of the Cambridge Study in Delinquent Development*, London: Heinemann.

West, D.J. and Farrington, D.P. (1977) *The Delinquent Way of Life: Third Report of the Cambridge Study in Delinquent Development*, London: Heinemann.

Whyte, W.F. (1943) *Street Corner Society: The Social Structure of an Italian Slum*, Chicago: University of Chicago Press.

Williams, H.W. (1949) *South London*, London: Robert Hale.

Willis, P.E. (1977) *Learning to Labour: How Working Class Kids get Working Class Jobs*, Farnborough, Hants: Saxon House.

Willmott, P. (1966) *Adolescent Boys of East London*, London: Routledge & Kegan Paul.

Wilson, H. (1975) 'Juvenile Delinquency, Parental Criminality and Social Handicap', *British Journal of Criminology* Vol 15, No 3, July, pp 241–50.

Wilson, H. (1980) 'Parental Supervision: A Neglected Aspect of Delinquency', *British Journal of Criminology* Vol 20, No 3, July, pp 203–35.

Wilson, H. and Herbert, G. (1978) *Parents and Children in the Inner City*, London: Routledge & Kegan Paul.

Wolfgang, M.E., Figlio, S., and Sellin, T. (1972) *Delinquency in a Birth Cohort*, Chicago: University of Chicago Press.

Yancey, L. and Eriksen, E.P. (1979) 'The Antecedents of Community: The Economic and Institutional Structure of Urban Neighbourhoods', *American Sociological Review* Vol 44, April, pp 253–62.

Young, M. and Willmott, P. (1957) *Family and Kinship in East London*, London: Routledge & Kegan Paul, 1962 Harmondsworth: Pelican.

Zweig, F. (1961) *The Worker in Affluent Society: Family Life and Industry*, London: Heinemann.

Index